Praise for
The Practice

"Barb Schmidt is a transformational leader who fearlessly shares her authentic truth. In her book, *The Practice*, Barb offers readers life-changing spiritual guidance in an easy to follow format. What makes this book so magnificent is that Barb has infused her own stories and struggles to help readers connect and learn."

—**Gabrielle Bernstein**, *New York Times* bestselling author of *May Cause Miracles*

"One of the most common questions I am asked is how to integrate a spiritual practice with daily life. Barb Schmidt's small book supplies a very practical answer by setting out clear guidelines on how to transform our daily round into a spiritual path. This includes instruction on being present in the moment with focused attention, mantra recitation, and opening the heart to all others in gratitude and loving kindness. This beautiful book is filled with practical advice and inspirational instruction.

"Having embarked on a spiritual search an' ̶ ̶ ̶ ̶ ̶ ̶ ̶ cerely for many years, Barb Schmidt ̶ ̶ ̶ ̶ ̶ ̶ ligence and harmonious kir' ̶ ̶ ̶ ̶ book is the result of her ov ̶ ̶ ̶ ̶ anyone—irrespective of relig ̶ ̶ ̶ ̶ ̶ ̶ ̶ ̶ ̶ ̶ ̶ ̶ ed in travelling the spiritual path."

—**Jetsunma** ̶ ̶ ̶ **almo**, Buddhist nun, author of *Into the Heart of Life*, teacher and founder of the Dongyu Gatsal Ling Nunnery in Himachal Pradesh, India

"The effectiveness of this book lies in the sincere and encouraging manner in which Barb Schmidt shares her insights and suggestions for meditation and other spiritual practices that she has personally learned from a wide range of spiritual traditions and teachers. She provides practical suggestions to help readers cooperate with the challenges and graces that flow from a quiet, patient commitment to meditation. Those who accept her invitation to begin a lifelong, daily practice of contemplation will be grateful for the interior transformations that will occur as meditation radiates out into their lives, helping them to become a healing presence in the world."

—**James Finley, Ph.D.**, Thomas Merton scholar,
author of *Christian Meditation*

"Barb Schmidt writes in such a gentle, relaxed conversational style that it felt to me as if she were taking me by the hand and introducing me to the world of meditation and spiritual healing that she knows so well. And the quotes are just perfect—introduced at just the right time and in an unobtrusive way. It is a very moving piece of work."

—**Doris Kearns Goodwin**, Pulitzer Prize–winning
American biographer, historian, and political commentator

"For many the world is a noisy, chaotic, overwhelming place. We are incessantly bombarded by stimuli via technology, mobility, and media. Today we must address hundreds of decisions that our grandparents couldn't even have contemplated. Couple that with the human tendency to worry, overanalyze, and fret, and suddenly the mind can become something like Times

Square on New Year's Eve—a lot of energy expended, but it doesn't get you anywhere.

"Barb Schmidt has traveled that course and came to understand that there had to be a better way to journey through life. She found a path that affords tranquility, peace of mind, and serenity; a path that nurtures the soul and elevates the spirit. Her book is a sincerely honest and candid tale of her discoveries. It invites readers to find their own pathway. *The Practice* is a template for a purposeful, happier, and fulfilling life."

—**Dan Baker, Ph.D.**, author of *What Happy People Know*

"*The Practice* is a wonderful spiritual book linking practical wisdom with daily mindful routines to learn to live in the moment. Barb Schmidt's extensive experience as a spiritual sojourner shines throughout the book. Her clear and concise method provides powerful tools for readers to train the mind to live a peaceful life.

"As a founder of the organization Peaceful Mind Peaceful Life, Barb Schmidt has presented a multitude of workshops over the years on The Practice, many as part of the Peace Studies Program at Florida Atlantic University. She led thousands of participants, providing them spiritual tools to engage with The Practice and learn the interconnectedness between peace in the world and peaceful lives as humans. As the Director of the Peace Studies Program, I participated in most of her workshops, and with each one increasingly realized how easy yet powerful The Practice is, and how learning to lead a peaceful life positively affects my own mindful routines. 'The Practice' is now *my* daily 'practice' for living in the moment, for attaining inner peace, for being part of bringing peace in the world."

—**Noemi Marin, Ph.D.**, director, School of Communication and Multimedia Studies, Florida Atlantic University (former director of Peace Studies Program, FAU), author of *After the Fall*

"Barb Schmidt is one of the most truly beautiful people I've ever met. Her beauty springs from a source within herself, endowing her with qualities that stand the test of time—patience, understanding, self-knowledge, serenity, and compassion, to name a few. She's on a quest to discover ways to tap into the most powerful, positive, life-affirming forces in the universe, and in this wonderful book she invites us to join her on that deeply rewarding journey.

"I've spent most of my life coaching young men who want to win football games. As any good coach will tell you, there's much more to it than that. The characteristics that make players winners on the field can also make them winners in life. Staying positive in the face of adversity, digging deep to find new wells of inner strength, having faith in yourself and the people around you, visualizing success—all of these things profoundly influence a person's ability to move calmly and confidently through life, savoring its joys and weathering its storms.

"The best, and most beautiful, thing about Barb is her passion for sharing her outlook with others. I'm happy and grateful to call Barbara 'coach,' and as you read *The Practice* I'm sure that you'll be, too.

—**Howard Schnellenberger**, founding football coach and ambassador-at-large, 1998–present, Florida Atlantic University; University of Miami national champions coach, 1983

THE
PRACTICE™

Simple Tools for Managing Stress, Finding Inner Peace, and Uncovering Happiness

BARB SCHMIDT

Founder, Peaceful Mind Peaceful Life

Health Communications, Inc.
Deerfield Beach, Florida

www.hcibooks.com

**Library of Congress Cataloging-in-Publication Data
is available through the Library of Congress**

© 2014 Barb Schmidt

ISBN-13: 978-07573-1798-9

Publisher: Health Communications, Inc.
 3201 S.W. 15th Street
 Deerfield Beach, FL 33442–8190

The illustration of the mind on page 59 is by Jessica Chin Fong
Cover illustration and design by Larissa Hise Henoch
Interior design and formatting by Lawna Patterson Oldfield

For

Mary Cormier

my friend, my angel

"A THOUGHT WHICH
IS WELL GUARDED
BY A CONTROLLED MIND
BRINGS HAPPINESS."

—*B.K.S. Iyengar*

CONTENTS

PREFACE

"**People are just as happy as** they make up their minds to be." When I heard this quote by Abraham Lincoln, I was in grade school. I could not understand what my mind had to do with being happy, but I really wanted to know. To me, *happy* meant having all the things I had read about in the fairy tales and had seen in movies. It also meant having a close, unshakable connection with God. I desperately wanted to be happy, but I just wasn't. I began searching for happiness everywhere.

That was a long time ago. Today, my life's quest is about *being* happy, whole, loving, and loved and to spread the message that we are all capable of living a magnificent, purposeful, and happy life by tapping into the inner peace and strength we have within us every day. In my nearly ten years of giving workshops and seminars on the topic of peace, I have been helping people understand that our minds are at the root of our unhappiness, as Abraham Lincoln suggested. If we can learn to train our minds, we can be happy. When we know the deep happiness that comes from within, we can better manage the daily stresses in our lives and live a calmer, more present existence.

I am not a clinical expert, a guru, or a mental health professional. I am a self-taught spiritual teacher who has spent her life training with many of the great modern-day teachers, as well as studying the texts of many of the incredible masters, mystics, and saints of the past. I have taken all that I have learned and practiced for nearly thirty years and developed a daily spiritual routine I call The Practice. The Truths I talk about with regard to The Practice are not new. They are a compilation of the Truths and wisdom from many of the great religions and teachings. I have simply structured all of this into an easy-to-implement daily routine that can bring peace, meaning, and happiness to anyone's life.

Through my workshops, website, and now this book, I share The Practice with many different types of people: those who have never meditated or followed spiritual disciplines but feel the pull toward leading a more meaningful, happier life; those who have been asking themselves, *What is my purpose?* and *Why am I here?*; those who have a meditation practice and lead a present life but are looking for tools to add structure and mindfulness throughout the day; and those who already have a serious practice but find some of the practical suggestions in The Practice helpful in furthering them along their path. Whatever category you fall into, my wish for you is that you find this book useful in a way that speaks to you.

But who am I? How did I become the happy and confident person I am today? My quest for peace and happiness began as far back as I can remember. As a child, I believed there had to be more to life than what I had—that there was something I had to find or do or be. I often found myself wondering, *Should I be a nun . . . or a queen? Which will make me happier?* Of course, I didn't end up being either of those things. It was more about what they represented to me—a spiritual life versus a material life. I struggled with the thought that I could have only one or the other.

I was the oldest of five children in a low-income, Catholic family with parents who struggled with many challenges, including alcoholism. As a result, I felt responsible from very early on. I strove for perfection in everything I did—at school, in the family, in church, and at work. I found myself trying to keep very busy and to be the best at everything. I believed this would make me happy and that my life would be perfect. But we all know there is no such thing as perfection, so I ended up feeling "less than," alone, and unloved—always on the outside looking in.

Among the four jobs I had in high school, working at McDonald's was my favorite. I made many friends, the people in management liked me and valued my hard work, and I felt appreciated and needed. I took great pride in my role as a McDonald's employee, and, in fact, my self-worth was vested in that job. So when I was offered a manager's position following my high school graduation, I accepted without thinking twice—in lieu of college, much to my parents' displeasure.

Within five years, I owned my first McDonald's franchise, which was made possible by a business facilities–lease program that McDonald's Corporation offered to employees whom they recognized as having the high standards and values necessary to be successful but lacking the capital. In the years that followed, I put every bit of my effort into creating an incredible career.

According to our society's measurements, I had achieved all the external things I could possibly want: six franchises, a handsome husband, a social life, money, and an attractive appearance, too. However, despite my obvious outward success, I did not feel happy. Most of the time I felt incomplete. *Is this what happiness is?* I wondered. *Maybe I am doing something wrong.* I would fall asleep at night, feeling empty and alone. My husband at the time said to me one day, "You have *everything.* Is there *anything* that will make you happy?" This remark made me even sadder. *What was wrong with me?*

One October morning in 1984, I read an article in the paper that talked about Karen Carpenter's battle with anorexia, which she had lost on February 4, 1983. I listened to the music of the Carpenters (a duo with her brother, Richard) all the time in high school, so I had been deeply saddened when she died a year earlier, but oddly enough, the cause of her death did not register with me at the time.

Now, more than a year later, reading about how she had lost her battle with this eating disorder—a subject that was rarely, if ever, covered by the media—shook me to my core. As I read on, it dawned on me that I too had an eating disorder: mine was bulimia. I started to cry, and a voice inside me said, *You must get help.* The voice was strong, loud, and firm, so I felt moved to listen.

The very next day, I checked myself into a treatment center. From the moment I arrived for my six-week stay, I felt safe, accepted, and loved. I started to take great comfort in sharing my thoughts and feelings in individual and group therapy. I had a beautiful sense that I was not alone, and I connected with people from all walks of life. I had a fabulous roommate; we bonded instantly and remain close today.

The treatment center introduced me to the Twelve Steps, for which I will always be grateful for my recovery. With each week that passed, I found even greater strength and wisdom in the support I was receiving. It was there that I became immersed in inspirational reading and spiritual instruction, finding comfort, hope, and strength in the teachings. By the end of my stay, I had an incredible desire to live a more spiritual, more meaningful life.

I left the treatment center happy and excited about my life and its potential to evolve. Not too long after my recovery, on November 4, 1985, I gave birth to my beautiful daughter, Michelle. Becoming a mother unearthed in me many feelings, but the greatest was a deep understanding of the true meaning of selfless service and love. Motherhood is such an amazing gift! I instantly felt more patient and more loving, and my inner voice urged me to start looking for a way to be of further service and give back to the world. So, in 1988, I cofounded Ronald McDonald Children's Charities of South

Florida and remained its president until 1996 (the same year I sold my McDonald's franchises).

During my years as president, I continued seeking spiritual inspiration and found it from teachers such as Scott Peck and his book *The Road Less Traveled,* Deepak Chopra and his book *Ageless Body, Timeless Mind,* and Marianne Williamson and her book *A Return to Love.* I went on several retreats with these inspiring teachers and found great support for living the life I wanted to live.

Moving on from my association with McDonald's marked a major transition for me. I knew that it signified a new chapter in my life. I felt sad—nostalgic, really—but very excited about what would be next. I felt it was time for me to find my life's passion and to be of service. My voice within said, *You are ready. Find what you have come here to do and do it.*

Having made inspirational reading a regular part of my life, I came across the book *Living Buddha, Living Christ* by Thich Nhat Hanh. The title intrigued me. I was raised Catholic and was now hungry for learning about all religions and everything spiritual. In the book, I was introduced to the concept that meditation and mindfulness could lead me to a deeper connection with God. The message touched my heart deeply. I went on two retreats with Thich Nhat Hanh, which paved the way for my serious search for a spiritual teacher to guide me to the life I longed to live. As a result of my experiences at these retreats and others, I became a vegetarian for spiritual reasons and remain so to this day.

The Yoga Sutras of Patanjali, written in the second century BC, became a major focus of my studies. Along with Jesus, the Buddha, Sri Ramakrishna, Swami Vivekananda, Saint Francis of Assisi, Rumi, Saint Teresa of Avila, and Gandhi, Patanjali is one of my most influential teachers. My modern-day teachers have included Scott Peck, Thomas Merton, Deepak Chopra, Marianne Williamson, Thich Nhat Hanh, Eknath Easwaran, His Holiness the Dalai Lama, Pema Chödrön, Jetsunma Tenzin Palmo, Caroline Myss, James Finley, and now most recently Gabrielle Bernstein. Since 1985, I have been on more than a hundred retreats with these teachers.

What I realize now—and really knew back then—is that I was not just looking for inspiration from a teacher. I was looking for somebody to tell me what to do, show me the answer, and lead the way. In 1998, I thought I had found the answer to living a deeply grounded, spiritual life in a well-respected but very rigid meditation community that followed the teachings of one particular spiritual teacher. I followed that path for ten years, devoting my time and finances to the organization's well-being. After a time, I began to feel stifled by the rigidity of the organization and by my feelings of separation. Following a series of disheartening events, my voice within said, *It is time for you to move on.*

Leaving this community, which had become the center of my life for so many years, was difficult. Gratefully, I had accumulated such a wealth of spiritual inspiration and discipline that when faced with the question of what was next, the answer came to me easily one morning in my meditation through the words of Swami Vivekananda: "You have to grow from the inside out. No one can teach you; no one can make you spiritual. There is no other teacher but your own soul."

I came out of my meditation that morning feeling ready to be a teacher, while continuing to be a student. Yogi Bhajan's words took on new life: "I came here to create teachers." I felt confident and wildly alive knowing that I could move forward in my spiritual journey, turning within to my Beloved, my Inner Guide. I had changed myself. I was now a happy, confident, and strong person, and it was now my duty and responsibility to be a light and begin the work of helping to change the world. As Mahatma Gandhi says so magnificently: "Be the change you wish to see in the world."

As a result of my fifty-plus years in life, I have found a way of living my everyday life that brings me a deep sense of happiness, security, love, confidence, and peace—a deep, unshakable connectedness to my Beloved. I know I can handle all the ups and downs of life, lead a happy and fulfilling life, and ultimately leave this world better than when I arrived. When someone asked me recently during one of my talks, "Barb, what do you define as being happy?" I remembered a time when I did not know what it meant to be happy. But now I smiled, because the answer came effortlessly:

> For me, happiness is knowing that I am strong, capable, confident, secure, loving, and compassionate; it is knowing that within me is everything I need to handle whatever life sends my way, and that not only will I be okay, I will thrive.

Today, I am a teacher and a seeker of knowledge, inspiration, Truth, and, ultimately, the unity of all beings. I know at a deep level what all the great saints, masters, and mystics know: I must become my own teacher to live my life authentically, confidently, and mindfully. This knowing within me is the support and happiness I had been looking for all those years.

While this book will teach you how to incorporate The Practice into your own life, I share this information with you so that you can experience that your greatest teacher is within you—discover this Truth, and you will change yourself.

In every workshop I give, I always say that we are incredible human beings. I know that each of us is truly meant to do extraordinary things with our lives—even when those things may seem ordinary. The Practice helps us develop the discipline to go within each day and to be present to the ordinary moments of our day. When we do this regularly, we begin to understand that we hold the key to our own peaceful mind. It is our peaceful mind that leads to a happy and peaceful life . . . and ultimately to a beautiful, loving, more peaceful world. It is my deep desire today that all beings know how amazing they are and find wholeness, love, and peace in their lives. Be Happy.

INTRODUCTION

*"Our mind with its incessant stream
of thoughts, memories, opinions, hopes and
fears is our constant companion, from
which we cannot escape even in our dreams.
So it makes sense to cultivate a worthy
travel companion for our journey."*

—Jetsunma Tenzin Palmo

When I listened to **Tenzin Palmo** talk about the mind on a retreat in 2010, I completely understood what she meant about our mind being our closest companion. It is *always* with us. I also remember thinking that this companion of ours can often sound like an annoying broken record, harping on the same old complaints and concerns.

Listening to all the mind's judgments, worries, planning, memories, and fantasies is stressful and drains our energy, interferes with our ability to be present, and keeps us focused on outward things that are supposed to make us feel happy. When we are so focused on what is going on in our minds, we are not able to function at our highest level or fully appreciate our blessings. We look at the state of the world and all its problems, all *our* problems, and we question how we can be happy with all that is going on. We wonder about the injustice of it all and often lose patience with others and ourselves for not being able to "make things right" and "just be happy." Living this way can cause us a great deal of suffering and a lot of stress.

So we look for distractions, outward things, to make us feel better. In our society, there is no shortage of them. The media bombards us with flashy images and false promises. These external influences somehow sink their hooks into our hearts and convince us that we need them to find the happiness and fulfillment we are longing for. From very early on, we have been taught by society that if we "get this" and "achieve that," life will be great and we will be happy. But no matter how much we accumulate or use to make us feel better or forget, we still feel as if something is missing. "Things" cannot make us happy, and even though we know this deep down, we still hope that maybe this one more thing will be "the thing" that will do it for us.

Here is the good news: The potential to be happy is right inside of us—there is nothing we need to find and then figure out how to get. Nothing we seek on the outside can compare to that. We might think we have found something or someone who "completes" us, that gives us the "wholeness" we are in search of, but we all know from experience that feelings based on changing circumstances do not last. People age and die, situations end, tragedy strikes, natural disasters occur, things get used up or are no longer useful, and the list goes on and on. However, in reality, what *never* changes is within each one of us, and this is the part that makes us whole.

Carl Jung wrote, "Your vision will become clear when you look into your heart. Who looks outside dreams, who looks inside awakens." When our hearts awaken to this Truth, we can all say with deep sincerity and knowing, "I am complete." When we live from within, we will know peace and happiness. The daily stresses of life will be more manageable, and our days will be more fulfilling.

When I heard the Dalai Lama speak at Florida Atlantic University as part of the Peace Studies Program in 2010, he repeated a sentiment that he often shares: "Life is meant to be happy." We are meant to be happy. Our minds con us into wondering what that means. *Are we happy? Why aren't we happy?* We think it is a feeling we sometimes have: "How do you feel?" someone asks, and the other person replies, "Well, I was happy yesterday, but today I'm not so happy because this happened to me. It was so stressful!" That sort of happiness is like riding a roller coaster—fleeting at best.

When the great masters and teachers talk about happiness, they are talking about that underlying sense of joy, peace, and security that we will find inward when we seek it through stillness and by being present to the moments of our lives. This place of stillness is within each one of us, and we can tap into it by having a spiritual practice that quiets the mind—not to get rid of it, but to enrich and nourish it and teach it to listen inwardly. "The word that comes out of listening changes hearts," says my friend James Finley, a Thomas Merton scholar. This is a profound Truth: change happens within.

The idea is to cultivate our minds the way we would a garden, by planting the plants we want, tending to them regularly, and keeping the ground fertile. When we do this daily, we start to align our mind, body, and heart so that each part of us works together in unity with a beautiful rhythm. This is what The Practice helps us do.

We are like a magnificent tree with an incredible root system. Even though we cannot see what is going on underground, we know that the root system is vital to the tree's ability to thrive. The roots are its strength, its foundation, and what gives the tree its nourishment. And the same is true for us. Even if we cannot see it, our strength and nurturing is there inside us, providing us with everything we need to thrive.

THE PRACTICE

The Practice, as taught in this book, is a set of practical tools that can be used throughout the day to guide us along our life's path. It is a compilation of the great Truths taught by authentic teachers and masters throughout the centuries from various religious and spiritual traditions. The Practice creates the following three-part framework around which to live our magnificent lives:

1. **Waking Up**
   Meditation

2. **Living Present**
   Sacred Mantra
   Focused Attention
   Reading for Inspiration

3. **Letting Go**
   Reflection

Simply stated, these tools are meant to help us cultivate a peaceful mind so that we can lead the happy, loving, mindful, purposeful lives we are looking to have—the magnificent lives we are meant to live. They provide us with structure in our day so that we can take the necessary time to go within and bring our mind, body, and heart into alignment and ground ourselves. When we go inward, we cultivate the beautiful qualities of acceptance, gratitude, patience, compassion, strength, and courage. These are the talents that help us deal with the difficulties in our lives and help break down the obstacles that hold us back from tapping into our source of love, peace, and happiness.

Why did I call this daily routine The Practice? Martha Graham defines the word *practice* beautifully: "Practice means to perform, over and over again in the face of all obstacles, some act of vision, of faith, of desire." Cultivating our minds—reining in the thoughts that interfere with our happiness and inner peace—takes practice.

The keywords in Graham's definition are *over and over again*. This means we need to do something consistently to be able to enjoy the benefits. This is not something we do until we get it right, and then everything will be perfect. No, The Practice is not a panacea or a quick fix. We know life is not perfect and that expecting it to be that way is a big obstacle to inner peace. "It is the journey, not the destination," it has been said. So to remain on the path, we must "perform, over and over again in the face of all obstacles."

The Practice is not a religion. It can be a complement to any religious or spiritual practice, or it can stand entirely on its own. People who are looking to deepen their connection to their innermost selves can incorporate The Practice into their daily lives. There is no need to have meditated previously to start enjoying the benefits of this spiritual discipline. Likewise, those who already engage in meditation and other spiritual pursuits may find the framework I offer here helpful for structuring their day in such a way that there is always time for looking within to regain balance and clarity.

We do not have to go anyplace special to do The Practice, and we certainly do not have to live in seclusion to lead a spiritual and happy life. We have everything we need right where we are to live a life with depth, meaning, and "spirit." The Practice helps us look at the world and ourselves differently, allowing us to live life from a fresh vantage point. We learn how to tap into our Inner Guide, our Source, to connect with God, of our understanding (from the Eleventh Step of Alcoholics Anonymous: "God as we understood him").

By going within, we align our mind, body, and heart, but we do this with awareness that we are not perfect; life is not perfect. Although we cannot expect to stay in alignment all day long, we do know how we feel when our spirit, our essence, radiates love and confidence. That is the beauty of The Practice: when we recognize that we are coming out of alignment and stress is getting the best of us, we can take a few deep breaths to bring ourselves back to center. I like to call this "checking in with ourselves." We are human, so we *will* go off track. The question is how quickly do we recover and get back into alignment? Some days it may take minutes, some days it may take hours, and there may even be times when it may take days or months. The whole point here is to keep practicing and continue along our path. When we live life by checking within periodically, we are better able to make choices and take actions that bring us more joy and less stress. I call this "living life from the inside out."

HOW TO USE THIS BOOK

In the first three chapters of this book, you will be guided through the three parts of The Practice: Waking Up, Living Present, and Letting Go. We begin with a morning meditation and remain aware of the peace we tapped into as the day progresses through the repetition of a Sacred Mantra, practicing Focused Attention, Reading for Inspiration, and Reflection at the end of the day. Each chapter concludes with

"Parting Thoughts" and "Takeaway Seeds." These are key points from the chapter that are helpful to keep in mind as you go about your day. In the final chapter, you will have an opportunity for deepening your experience of The Practice with practical exercises.

After you have read through this book once, you can keep it close by in case you have any questions or would like to look at a part of The Practice more closely, so that little by little you may integrate it more fully into your life. My wish is that you will find this book a faithful companion on your life's journey.

In these pages, I share with you what I have learned through my nearly thirty years of study and practice. I discovered very early on that although it is so incredibly inspiring and necessary to hear and read what others have to say about the spiritual journey and about life, it is not until we experience it for ourselves that we will know personally, on a deep level, what they are all talking about. No one can make that happen for us. As the Buddha said, "We ourselves must walk the path." We must walk the walk and discover who we truly are.

The Benefits of The Practice

When we regularly take the steps to go within each morning, stay present throughout the moments of our daily routine, and let go of our attachments to the day when it comes to a close, we will find that The Practice is helping us to do the following:

- ⤜ Recognize that our everyday life is our spiritual life
- ⤜ Remove the obstacles that interfere with inner peace
- ⤜ Manage stress and cultivate more patience, empathy, and compassion
- ⤜ Have more courage when facing fears and making changes
- ⤜ Overcome habitual behaviors and make better choices
- ⤜ Get out of reaction mode and take time to consider our responses
- ⤜ Reduce negative thinking and ease feelings of anxiety, worry, and stress
- ⤜ See the blessings beneath life's more difficult experiences
- ⤜ Awaken our heart and uncover our truest self residing within
- ⤜ Know a deep feeling of wholeness, that we are complete

CHAPTER 1

WAKING UP

Tapping into Our Inner Source of Strength and Wisdom

*"Meditation is one of the ways a spiritual
man keeps himself awake."*

—Thomas Merton

Each day is a gift. There is no guarantee we will ever have another one. When we look at it from this perspective, we can better appreciate how fortunate we are when we open our eyes in the morning. But with everything going on in our lives and the world, it is easy to wake up and immediately shift into autopilot and begin thinking about how to accomplish everything on our never-ending to-do list. Sometimes even before the alarm goes off, our minds have us plotting and planning how we are going to make it through our day so that we can finally relax at the end of it. Toss in all the concerns and worries we have to carry around, and by the time we get out of bed, we are already exhausted.

Is this how we really want to live our precious lives? For me, I can emphatically say *no,* and I would venture to say you would agree. Most of us think we just do not have a choice— this is the way we have been programmed; it is the way things are. But I am here to affirm that we do have a choice in how we live every moment of every day.

This different, more mindful way to approach the day—a way that energizes, empowers, and inspires us—is through morning meditation. In the first part of The Practice, Waking Up, instead of hitting the ground running, we start each morning by setting the intention to be present throughout the day. Instead of "wake up and go," we "wake up and stop." It sounds contrary to everything we have been taught, but it is an essential component of greeting the day at our best, on our terms . . . with a peaceful mind.

So the first action we do every morning in the framework of The Practice is meditate. Any misconceptions about meditation strictly being a practice for monks and nuns is addressed beautifully by Thich Nhat Hanh: "Meditation is not to escape from society, but to come back to ourselves and see what is going on. Once there is seeing, there must be acting. With mindfulness, we know what to do and what not to do to help." Meditation is about going within every morning to see what's "going on." It is a practice of going somewhere quiet to sit down and calm the mind of its rush of thoughts. In this sitting and quieting of the mind, we come in touch with a stillness within—we are "coming back to ourselves."

We connect with ourselves deep within like the roots of a tree grounding itself in the earth. This morning meditation helps us go inward and tap into the place that calms, centers, and empowers us. By connecting within, we align our mind, body, and heart. This alignment represents our spirit—our essence in the world; it helps us go out into our day feeling confident and strong. I have often heard it said, "The real world is not out there, it is in here." I say it this way: "When we go within, we discover that the inner world is just as real as the outer world." When we live this way, our outer world mirrors the serenity of our inner world beautifully. As I like to say in my workshops and seminars, "This is living our lives from the inside out."

By taking this quiet time, we give ourselves the wonderful opportunity to truly appreciate the beauty of having another day to spend on earth. When we wake up and our feet touch the ground, we have the opportunity to say to ourselves, "Wow, I am so glad to be alive! I am happy I have this day! Thank you for this gift of another day!" and really believe it.

Although I have been meditating since the early eighties, I have been consistently beginning my day with meditation for the past eighteen years. There was a time in my life when I believed I could think my way through life and that the body and the heart would "kind of just take care of themselves." I was mistaken. We need the mind, body, and heart all working together and supporting one another. By meditating, I am intentionally aligning my mind, body, and heart, which gives me a calmer and more peaceful mind, a healthier and stronger body, and a heart that awakens to life in the most beautiful ways.

Let's now take a look at how and when to meditate within the framework of The Practice, what you might experience during meditation, and why it is so important to begin the day with this peaceful practice.

THE WAKING UP MEDITATION

"Awake with a winged heart, and give
thanks for another day of loving."

—Kahlil Gibran

Meditation is about a lot of things, but simply, it is about relaxing our nervous system and calming our minds so that we can go within and listen to the "whisperings of our hearts." It gives us an opportunity to just be. In meditation, we are cultivating the sitting process of attentiveness, being present. It is a practice of directing our attention inward with a single-pointed focus. The intention is to achieve an inner sense of peace and a deep connection with oneself. During this time of stillness, we find an unwavering knowing that "all is well" deep in our hearts. This is the well of confidence and strength that we take into our outer world.

In The Practice, we sit in meditation first thing in the morning to quiet the mind so that we can tap into our inner guidance and center of peace. Starting the day in silence may seem odd at first because we have slept all night and now it "should" be time to get going. Most of us seem to be conditioned to want some outside stimulation when we arise. But let's face it: we live in a world that is going to give us that . . . all day long. So before we "get going," we take a few minutes to tap into the deep knowing within us so that we can greet the day in alignment, centered, and grounded.

When I first tried to meditate, I did not think it would ever be possible for the thoughts in my head to stop—even for a second. It actually occurred to me that maybe I was one of those people who could not meditate. I kept in mind what the inspiring Buddhist nun Jetsunma Tenzin Palmo says in her book, *Into the Heart of Life:* "Meditation is the art of quieting the mind so that the endless chatter that normally fills our consciousness is stilled." So little by little, I stuck with my meditation practice. I did not give in to what those thoughts were saying. I just let them come and go. And this is exactly what we are doing in meditation: we are training the mind to be in silence by letting thoughts come and go. In my opinion, if I can meditate, *anyone* can meditate!

These inspiring words of Saint Francis de Sales also give me great comfort and support: "If the heart wanders or is distracted, bring it back to the point quite gently and replace it tenderly in its Master's presence. And even if you did nothing during the whole of your hour but bring your heart back and place it again in Our Lord's presence, though it went away every time you brought it back, your hour would be very well employed." I continue to take Saint Francis de Sales's words to heart. They let me know that it is perfectly natural for the mind to have thoughts during meditation and that our practice is to simply allow them to come and go.

I will talk more about the challenges of dealing with our minds later in this chapter and throughout this book. For now, let us begin by taking a look at the practicalities of incorporating the Waking Up Meditation into your daily routine.

WHEN TO MEDITATE. Meditate first thing in the morning, before you engage the day. It is so easy to get caught up in the outside world if you decide to wait to meditate until after "everything" is done. If there are tasks you absolutely must do first, such as walk and feed the dog, take a shower, or have something to drink, go ahead and do that, but try to do so with a peaceful frame of mind. The point is to make a real effort to keep from engaging the outside world. For example, the morning news, your cell phone, and your computer can all wait. You will have all the time in the day to interact with the world.

Ideally, wake up early enough so that you are finished meditating by the time you would normally begin your outward routine. Figure out how much time you need and then back it up from there. For example, if you need to leave the house at 9:00 AM and it takes you an hour to get ready, wake up at 7:30 to give yourself uninterrupted time to meditate.

When my daughter was young, I would get up at 4:30 AM to allow myself my uninterrupted time in meditation. Then I could attend to her needs in the morning. When one of her friends spent the night, she commented on how organized and calm it was at our house in the morning. "You even have breakfast!" she said. You see, by starting the day with meditation, we set the tone for the entire day.

Today I no longer have to get up that early, but back then, it worked for me. So I encourage you to figure out what works best for you in your current situation. The keyword here is *current*. We are practicing living in the moment, and our lives are constantly changing, so recognizing this and being okay with change is a must. I have found that it is impossible to simultaneously be rigid and live in the present moment open and receptive to what life sends our way. The only thing you need to know for certain (and not change your mind about) is that you are making a decision, an intention, to meditate every morning. That is it! Everything else in life will come and go and change.

WHERE TO MEDITATE. Dedicate a quiet place in your home to practice your morning meditation. If you have a room to set aside for this purpose, that is wonderful but not necessary. A corner, a nook, or even just a chair or cushion will work. I meditate in the corner of my guest room, sometimes in a chair and sometimes on the floor. After many years of meditating every day, I listen to my body and sit in either place on any given morning.

In the early days, when you have made the decision to make meditation a way to start your day, I have found it important to have a specific space and routine. Remember, you are training the mind, and structure is perfect for doing that. The key is to establish a place in your home where the likelihood of your being disturbed is minimal during the meditation. If you choose your office or TV room for your meditation practice, your mind might entice you to forgo the meditation for a quick look at your e-mail or a news update. So be sure to pick a room or space that you do not associate with the outside world. Over time, the mind will become accustomed to the fact that this place, corner, or cushion is for meditation and will learn to quiet down in this space.

Although one aim of meditating regularly is to be able to reach that quiet state of mind no matter where you are or what is going on around you, this takes practice. In the beginning, sitting in the same place consistently each morning lets your mind know that it is time for meditation.

HOW LONG TO MEDITATE. Meditate for five to thirty minutes. I have found that thirty minutes is the ideal meditation time for me. But if you have never meditated before, you may find it difficult to sit that long, so it is perfectly okay to start with five minutes. At first, even a few minutes may seem like a long time. Just bear with it for a few days or weeks, and you will begin to notice that you actually may want to extend the time you are sitting. This quote by a View on Buddhism (www.viewonbuddhism.org) restates this concept beautifully: "One should realise that continuity in meditation is considered essential: better five minutes a day, every day, than two hours once a week. For example, five minutes in the morning are likely to become longer over time, and can easily become part of your everyday life."

Students often ask me, "How do we know when our meditation time is over?" Once you have been meditating regularly, you will just naturally know when your meditation is coming to a close. This is part of the deep knowing I talk about; it really is such a beautiful thing. But this may not be the case when you first begin, so it is okay to set a gentle timer—nothing blaring or so persistent that it becomes agitating to the mind and nervous system when it goes off. Today, cell phones and electronic tablets offer a variety of gentle alarm options. In my weekly meditation class at our local university, I use an app on my tablet that rings like a meditation bell when the session is over. This new era makes it so easy to meditate; I did not have a tablet back in the eighties.

POSTURE FOR MEDITATION. Sit in a chair, on a cushion, or on the floor with your head, neck, and spine in a straight line and with your back supported. Keep your hands in your lap, face up or face down, whichever feels comfortable. Avoid interlacing your fingers if you have a tendency to squeeze or clench your hands.

If you are sitting in a chair, your feet should be on the floor. If you are sitting on a cushion or on the floor, sit up against a wall. Back support helps ensure that your head, neck, and spine are in alignment, which helps your ability to breathe and stay focused during the meditation. Although some people choose to sit without back support, which is certainly fine, it is a must for me no matter how long I have been practicing. Without back support, you may end up slouching. This puts pressure on your lungs and interferes with your breathing, which can make you sleepy. Physical alignment also has the added benefit of contributing to the alignment of your mind, body, and heart.

You can sit in a lotus position on the floor like some of the great masters or yogis, but it is not necessary in order to meditate. Back in the eighties, I thought that this was the only way to sit for meditation, so when I learned that I could meditate in a chair and that my legs did not have to be crossed, I was elated!

The purpose of our morning meditation is to quiet the mind and leave the outside world behind for these precious minutes to access the stillness within before starting our day. We learn little by little to sit this way and "be." When we sit still, we learn to *be* still. However, if your body is aching during meditation due to an uncomfortable position, you will be distracted. Take some time to experiment with what feels right and works for your body. Depending on where you are in your life, you may find that certain meditation positions work better than others.

When I first started meditating, I preferred to sit in a chair. Back then I could not have imagined that I would have ever wanted to meditate on the floor. I used to tell people, "I am so glad we do not have to sit on the floor to meditate. I don't think my legs could make it!" Then, in 2000, a dear friend of mine introduced me to yoga, and it has changed so many parts of my life, but a major area has been the flexibility of my body. So now, in the last ten years or so, I use both the floor and a chair, but mostly I sit on the floor.

The point here is to try to get as comfortable as possible but not so comfortable that you fall asleep. If you fall asleep, the meditation is over.

Let me interject a thought here: there may be some instances in our lives when we find ourselves unable to sit up and meditate. I have had students ask me if they can meditate lying down. I have personally found this difficult; I always fall asleep. But please remember, this is your personal daily meditation practice. What works for me may not work for you, and vice versa. Always keep in mind that the purpose of meditation is to calm the mind, connect within, and reflect our inner world of strength, love, and knowing onto our outer world so that we can live the magnificent life we are called to live.

Remaining Awake During Meditation

When we first sit down for our meditation, we start at the surface level of consciousness, gradually going below the surface and slowly getting into the unconscious. Our nervous system starts to relax, and it is easy for sleep to come over us.

The first sign that you feel drowsy—maybe your head starts to nod or your shoulders start to droop—is the time to temporarily bring your body away from whatever it is resting on. If you need to, stand up for a few moments, open your eyes, and take a few deep breaths. Let the sleepiness pass and then sit back down, resuming your regular posture. I have found that acting immediately on the drowsiness when it first starts to come over me works. Not only do I *not* fall asleep for the rest of my meditation period, I am more alert.

But chances are you will fall asleep from time to time. I certainly have in my years of meditation practice. By falling asleep in meditation, I have learned that my meditation is over, so this gives me greater vigilance to do whatever is necessary to keep from falling asleep. Be kind to yourself and know that this is a valuable teaching. We all know that firsthand experience and knowledge is our greatest teacher.

As we move on to "How to meditate," I would like to share with you an incredibly visual quote by Kirpal Singh, a revered meditation teacher who passed away in 1974. He said, "Meditation is like closing one drawer and opening another. During the time of meditation, we merely put our thoughts and worldly problems in a drawer and close it."

Just visualize that for a moment. You walk into the room and sit on your chair, the floor, or a cushion. You have the intention that you are going to put everything in the outside world in a drawer and close it. Then open the drawer of meditation. When the meditation is over, you will reopen the drawer of your thoughts and worldly problems and handle them from a grounded place of strength, knowing, and peace.

HOW TO MEDITATE. Once you are comfortably seated, close your eyes. Begin by taking a few deep, cleansing, calming breaths. The breath connects our mind, body, and heart, bringing them into alignment. I love this quote by Sri Swami

Satchidananda in *The Yoga Sutras of Patanjali*: "We should always remember that the mind and the prana, or breathing, have close connections." Being aware of our breath is the pause that our mind needs to stop and bring us into the moment. We are setting aside this precious time in our day to meditate, and a few deep breaths helps us connect with that intention.

You can choose from various meditation techniques. If you are already using one that is working for you, please continue it. But if you do not have a practice or you would like to try something new, in the Waking Up Meditation you begin by focusing your mind on an object. An object is simply something you choose to have your mind focus on rather than trying to clear your mind completely. My recommendation is that you choose a verse, a prayer, a sacred text, a Sacred Mantra (see p. 62), or the breath. If you are selecting a prayer, a verse, or a sacred text, make sure to choose one that is positive and uplifting.

Here is a great visual of what the object can do: In India the elephants walk the streets with their *mahouts* (riders). It is the nature of the elephant's trunk to constantly move and sway—just as it is the nature of our minds to constantly think. When the elephant is walking through the narrow market-lined streets, its trunk could easily wreak great havoc. So the *mahout* gives the elephant a stick to hold in its trunk. Once the trunk is holding the stick, the elephant can walk freely and easily through the street with great pride. The stick is the object for slowing the movement of the elephant's trunk. The verse, Sacred Mantra, or breath is the object for our mind in meditation. When we meditate daily, we "walk through the streets of our lives" with great strength and confidence. I love elephants, and this beautiful analogy has helped me in my meditation practice.

Keeping your eyes closed, begin your meditation by silently repeating your Sacred Mantra (see page 171). Then start to recite to yourself your chosen verse, text, or prayer (one that you have memorized or already know by heart). Repeat it silently and slowly for the length of your meditation. You may notice that a point will come during your meditation that the attention—concentration on your breath, verse, or mantra—may "fall away" (just naturally cease), and you are left with a quiet mind. This is the "peace that passes all understanding."

Remember the whole point in meditation is not to stop the thoughts in the mind; it is to notice the thoughts and, without engaging them, let them pass through your mind. This is why we choose an object to focus on, just like the *mahout* who gives the elephant a stick to hold in its trunk. When you focus your mind on an object, you are less likely to get caught in your thoughts. And when the mind does wander, which it will inevitably do, refocusing on the object is a way to bring your mind back to the present and on your intention to meditate. For example, to keep from engaging the thoughts that are coming, focus on your breath. Put your attention entirely on your breath as you inhale and exhale. The breath becomes the object, and you let the thoughts come and go.

This is what works for me: a combination of my Sacred Mantra, my breath, and selected verses. I have been doing this for years, and although I have tried other types of meditation, this is right for me. Remember, this is *your* meditation practice, so determine for yourself what object keeps you the most focused and present during your meditation period and stick with it. This constancy during your meditation translates beautifully in the outer world as living in the present, being awake to every moment.

As distractions come during meditation (these include outside noises as well as thoughts in your mind), just continue to gently keep your attention on your chosen object. As long as there are no emergency sirens blaring in the background, there really is no need to acknowledge outside noises. The same is true for your thoughts. Let them come and go; do not engage them. This means that if your mind starts wondering about things, gets stuck in a memory, or asks you questions, do not respond to it. If your mind starts telling you that you do not have time to be sitting here doing this, simply let the thought go. Do not argue with it. The thoughts are trying to engage you; so just let them pass and return to your object. I love this visual image I once heard described during my yoga class: "Think of the thoughts as white clouds in the sky and your mind as the blue sky; gently let the clouds pass by."

Here is an example: as you are meditating, the thought *I'm hungry* may come up. Let the thought rise, watch it pass through your mind like a cloud, and then let it float away. If you engage the thought, you might begin wondering what you will have for dinner that evening. You may then start thinking that you will need to go to the supermarket. Then you begin to wonder how you will fit grocery shopping into your day. This is getting caught up in the thought. Instead, when the thought comes up or when you realize you are engaging it, just remind yourself that you are meditating and bring your mind gently and compassionately back to your object. This is meditation.

When we meditate by focusing our attention on an object, we need to keep in mind that this is simply a tool (the stick being held in the elephant's trunk), which is meant to help us to "dig" into our consciousness so that we can go deeper. The idea is not to concentrate on the object for the sake of the object, but to use it as a tool. Once you discover what works for you, just be sure to "stick" with your method. Of course, you are bound to hit rocks (and even some boulders!) from time to time, but just keep digging toward that place of silence, strength, and peace within you.

After all, meditation practice really is all about the practice, not about the result. Going into the practice of meditation thinking, *I'm going to see a light* or *I'm going to hear a sound* or *I'm going to still my mind completely*, or any other expectations we may have in the mind, will only hinder the practice. The peace and mindfulness you gain from having meditated will show up in your daily life when you see that you are patient instead of anxious and stressed, loving instead of short-tempered, and compassionate instead of judgmental. Really, the idea here is just to sit down and be. So often in our lives we are too busy to be, and our practice here is perfect training. The only thing you need to do is bring your mind back to the moment each time it wanders away. Remember what Saint Francis de Sales taught us: "Even if you did nothing but bring your heart back, though it went away every time

you brought it back, your hour would be very well employed."
And that is it. Staying with it, not giving in to the urge to get
up and go is the idea when you first begin. Just following
through on your commitment to stay there for your specified
amount of time is monumental.

♦ ♦ ♦

When the gentle reminder signals that the meditation is
over, your first inclination may be to hop right up and get
going. We can all relate to that feeling because we are so good
at doing rather than just being. It takes practice to be still. So,
instead, when your meditation is over, you might want to consider ending with a personal prayer, a moment of silence, or a
few words of gratitude. I end with "My Beloved, thank you for
my life today. Please grant me the grace of unshakable faith."

Whether you take this suggestion or just move on with
your day, the idea is to set the intention that you will carry this
peace, presence, and stillness with you as you go out into the
world. Leave your meditation space quietly, silently repeating
your Sacred Mantra as you enter the outside world. Now as
you go into the rest of your day, you will find yourself being
more present and more aware—awake.

CHALLENGES YOU
MAY ENCOUNTER

When you first begin a meditation practice, you might encounter a variety of obstacles. These obstacles include excuses such as these: *There is not enough time. This is too boring. It is so hard to sit still. I am not good at it. It is so difficult to stay awake.* And so on. Avoidance can be a problem for some: *I just can't bring myself to do it. I am always finding something else I need to do instead!* And then of course there is expectation: *Nothing is happening! I am never going to see "the light."* Procrastination is also a big one: *Oh, I will meditate tomorrow* or *I will start a practice next week.* If procrastination is something you experience, take note of this comment I heard on a retreat by my friend James Finley, who is a Thomas Merton scholar: "The world will not step aside so we can have our mystical life, so don't wait." These words go straight to the heart of procrastination.

I have found that no matter what obstacle may come your way—and we all have obstacles that the mind will throw at us—they can only be overcome by meditating anyway. That is it! Set a specific time and place, and do not deviate from your commitment to yourself to do it. Exercise your discipline, and "don't wait."

When I first began my meditation practice, I had this nagging feeling I was not doing it right. I was not sure what to expect, so when I thought "nothing" was happening, I began to think that I must be doing "it" wrong. There was that perfectionist in me coming out. So I just kept at it. Then, after a time of not giving up, I began to see the rough edges of my life softening. I saw that I could be patient in the midst of chaos and stress and loving in circumstances where I felt hurt, and kind in situations that tested me. My meditation truly was reflecting in my day; it actually was transforming me from the inside out. I heard on a retreat that Gandhi is thought to have said, "There is no failure in meditation; only the failure to meditate."

If you follow through on your intention to meditate every day and have faith in its benefits, it will become a regular part of your day—one that you would not miss for anything, like showering or brushing your teeth. Old excuses will just begin to fall away.

"Sit that way; and in the sitting still we learn to be still."

—James Finley

During our meditation, it is important to keep in mind that we each begin at the surface of where we presently are in life. This means that we are aware of some things about ourselves and unaware of other things. When we meditate regularly, we dig a little deeper into our subconscious mind each time. We are really digging down in there. Sometimes, the deeper we go, the more difficult it is to face what we are uncovering about ourselves. Feelings and memories have a way of rising to the surface. Let them come up. We must uncover everything in our unconscious.

My eating disorder, bulimia, which I mentioned in the preface, was all about eating to suppress my feelings. When I started to meditate, these feelings came up, overwhelmed me, and needed to be addressed with a professional. So if a memory or feeling is strong and difficult for you, which was the case for me, I am a firm believer in seeking out expert help by speaking with a counselor or advisor. Give yourself permission to feel the feelings, be kind and loving to yourself, knowing we all have our "stuff," and then decide for yourself what feels right for you. I was recently on a retreat with author Gabrielle Bernstein, who explains this beautifully: "Life's going to hurt, but it's meant to be felt. We're not trying to get over our issues; we're trying to go through them."

I have also found that speaking with like-minded friends about meditation, getting a meditation friend, and joining a meditation group can offer amazing support and a sense of community.

A Successful Meditation Practice

I believe that a "successful" meditation practice is not about seeing the light or reaching a state of nothingness. Although I have experienced a sense of profound peace and oneness in meditation, it is the deep insight and little things that come up for me during my meditation and throughout the day that I love most about my practice. I know my meditation is working when I can hear my inner self offering me guidance or the idea that I should think a little more deeply about something before I take an action or make a comment with my words.

With a consistent meditation practice, we truly start remaking ourselves from the inside out and begin embodying Gandhi's message of peace: anger transforms into compassion, hatred into love, impatience into patience, and insecurity into security.

THE IMPORTANCE OF QUIETING THE MIND WITH MEDITATION

I founded the not-for-profit organization Peaceful Mind Peaceful Life with the intention of bringing love and peace to the world. Yes, this is a pretty ambitious goal! I believe that with inner peace, we can have outer peace. The Dalai Lama's words here, which are found in *Inner and Outer Peace Through Meditation* by Rajinder Singh, embody the great importance of meditation in my life's work and for anyone looking to fully live a magnificent life: "There will be no lasting world peace unless individual human beings have some sense of inner peace. To create inner peace it is necessary to calm the mind, hence the importance of meditation."

When we sit in meditation every day, we are grounding ourselves in what is important; we stop identifying with our thoughts and we sit with a quietness and openness that helps us start to become aware and one with ourselves and all beings. Simply put, a quiet mind is a peaceful mind, which allows us to be present in the moment and able to function at our best.

Meditation is "practicing being present." To do this, we need to be able to clear away all of the mental clutter that is going on in our heads. Just what are we thinking about all the time? *Situations that have happened, might happen, or are currently happening and things like who said what, who did what, who is going to say or do what, and so on.* Thoughts like this keep us living outside ourselves, not in the present moment, and put us at the mercy of the world where virtually anything can throw us off balance and ruin our day.

Life is completely unpredictable, and all the thinking in the world is not going to give us the answers or the comfort and happiness we are seeking. We can plan and do our very best, which is what we are meant to do, but we have no control over the outcome or the result. We often end up using a good deal of our energy, attention, and time trying to control or change the outside world to make ourselves feel happy and content.

Anthony de Mello, a Jesuit priest, psychotherapist, and spiritual teacher of mine, advises us, "If it is peace you want, seek to change yourself, not other people. It is easier to protect your feet with slippers than to carpet the whole of the earth." Hearing this makes me chuckle because the truth is, we simply have no control over anything outside ourselves, and when our happiness is dependent on things in the outside world, it is destined to be short-lived.

What we *can* control, however, is what is going on inside us. We have control over how we act, how we live, and how we choose to respond to situations. When we act, respond, and live in a manner that is in alignment with our mind, body, and heart, we find the happiness and contentment we have been seeking. With a consistent meditation practice, our ability to exercise this control becomes stronger, and our minds are more inclined to let us take the driver's seat. This allows us the quiet time to cultivate a deeper understanding of ourselves and the world.

Living Awake

Through meditation we uncover a new level of awareness that allows us to see more possibilities than the ones we have become accustomed to. Our perspective widens. We start to become awake. "Buddha" means Awakened One, and I believe that when the Buddha talked about "living awake," he literally meant just that: knowing that we are alive, being mindful and aware of our decisions, and not just going through the conditioned behaviors of our lives, wondering from time to time, *Did I just do that? How did that happen? How did I end up here?* Living awake is knowing that, in every moment, we are making choices and existing in the present. We are totally focused on being here and being now.

When we go through life without mindfulness and operate on automatic pilot, we become entrenched in concepts such as "right and wrong" or "fair and unfair." In fact, we are so blasted with these concepts today that we forget they depend entirely on individual points of view. Of course I am not talking about the big debates and issues that are raging in the world today, which require separate discussions. I am talking about the smaller, manageable things in our daily lives: our individual perceptions and expectations of how people are supposed to act and how things are supposed to happen. William Shakespeare summed it up beautifully: "Expectation is the root of all heartache."

Close your eyes and ponder this quote for a few moments. *Expectation is the root of all heartache.* Wow! We all live with expectations of some kind or another, don't we? And when our expectations are not met, we may become disappointed, impatient, or aggravated with the people and the situations around us. That is heartache. This is what causes us a great deal of stress in our daily lives. Our mind might be so busy being offended that we forget to step back, take a breath, and tap into our inner source of patience and compassion, where we are better able to see the reality of the situation.

Of course I think it is perfectly normal for us to have expectations, but it is how much we allow them to go unchecked that can result in negative feelings. Let me share with you one of my own expectations that used to have the potential to "ruin" my day. Before you read on, remember that it truly is the small things we encounter on a daily basis that can catch us off guard. My example is of a *very small* annoyance over not having my expectation met.

There is a traffic light at the exit of my subdivision. There are two lanes: one for turning left or going straight, and one for turning right. When I approach this light, I usually want to turn right, but there is often a car in "my" lane wanting to go straight. My conditioned response is to get aggravated and impatient with the person in the car in front of me. I could start thinking, *Don't they realize that I have "got to go" and that they are wrong to be in this lane? This lane is for stopping on red and then going—not for going straight!* In short, I *expect* drivers to follow the rules of the road. When they do not, I could allow myself to become irate, which then could set a negative tone for the rest of my day. But thankfully and gradually, by starting my day in peace through meditation, I have trained my mind to stop and know that I have a choice. I take a breath that connects me within and instantly feel more patient and peaceful, and I am able to let the stressful feeling go. When I am patient, I am able to put things in a different perspective: this is not a life-or-death situation, I have no control over others, and waiting a few extra minutes is not the end of the world.

Patience is being willing and able to suppress restlessness or annoyance when faced with delay and to keep a clear head when confronted by opposition or difficulty. This is why the little irritations in our day are so perfect for practicing patience. When we are impatient, when our minds get so caught up in how things and other people should be, we take away our power to be present to life as it is. When we are angry, agitated, irritated, stressed, or frustrated, we simply do not have the ability to respond to events and others with a clear head.

Fortunately, regularly engaging in a meditation practice teaches us patience and tolerance as we train our minds to be still; in turn, we become more mindful and accepting of things as they are. Little by little we are able to let go of expectations, especially the small, irritating ones in our day that seem to carry a great deal of weight and importance.

When we are more mindful and patient, our expectations become preferences. It is simply a matter of changing our vocabulary. *We prefer that this happen next instead of expecting it.* This subtle shift in language reduces that sense of entitlement. Instead of wanting or needing something, we just prefer it. Not having something we prefer does not ruffle our feathers as much as not getting something we want, need, or expect. We have more patience for things that do not go our way. If our preference does end up happening, we are all that much more grateful. And if it does not, we can accept that gracefully.

For us to get to this acceptance, we find patience in the quiet of our meditation. Sri Swami Satchidananda said in *The Yoga Sutras of Patanjali,* "To understand that eternal peaceful You, the mind must be quiet; otherwise it seems to distract the truth." In our acceptance lies the Truth; in the Truth lies our happiness and peace.

THE HEALTH AND WELLNESS BENEFITS OF MEDITATION

Meditation is an accepted type of relaxation technique intended to bring about the "relaxation response"—a state in which breathing slows, blood pressure and oxygen consumption decrease, and an increased sense of well-being may be experienced, according to the definition of the National

Center for Complementary and Alternative Medicine.[1] According to the Mayo Clinic, "Relaxation techniques can help you cope with everyday stress and with stress related to various health problems, such as cancer and pain. . . . Practicing relaxation techniques can reduce stress symptoms by slowing your heart rate; lowering blood pressure; slowing your breathing rate; increasing blood flow to major muscles; reducing muscle tension and chronic pain; improving concentration; reducing anger and frustration; and boosting confidence to handle problems."[2]

I believe we can say that meditation is as good for our physical health as it is for our mental and spiritual well-being. I find reading the scientific research on meditation fascinating. Much of it is focused on the neurological changes that take place in the brain during or as a result of a regular meditation practice. One study, published in the journal *Brain Research Bulletin* and reported by *MITnews*, found that those who meditated for eight weeks "were better able to control a specific type of brain waves called alpha rhythms . . . activity patterns [that] are thought to minimize distractions, to diminish the likelihood stimuli will grab your attention."[3] And this is one of the main goals of a meditation practice: to be less distracted and more present in our lives, right?

In the *Canadian Journal of Psychiatry*, Dr. John L. Craven writes, "Controlled studies have found consistent reductions in anxiety in meditators. Several stress-related conditions have demonstrated improvement during clinical trials of meditation including hypertension, insomnia, asthma, chronic pain, phobic anxiety."[4] Meditation allows our bodies to relax. It is said that one hour of complete concentration in meditation is equal to four hours of sleep. After meditation, we have renewed strength, vitality, and energy.

The more science delves into the benefits of meditation, the more mainstream the practice is becoming. When I first started meditating in the 1980s, my friends thought I was a little "nuts," but by 2007, even Google had implemented a course for its employees that incorporated a meditation practice. This program, which was developed by the renowned Chade-Meng Tan, is now the subject of the book *Search Inside Yourself: The Unexpected Path to Achieving Success, Happiness (and World Peace)*.

Universities and medical centers across the nation are offering meditation classes to their students and patients and including meditation in their treatment plans. Duke University Hospital, for instance, teaches mindfulness meditation to its cardiac patients to help with stress management. According to *DukeHealth.org*, "Mindfulness meditation means tuning into the present moment and its accompanying sensations. One is aware of thoughts and emotions without being overwhelmed by them."[5]

While we can personally be aware of the benefits of our own meditation practice, we can also be assured that what we are doing is good for our health! With so many health experts espousing the benefits of relaxation and meditation, it is all the more reason to stop for a while each day and allow our bodies to take a breather and slow down—literally. This is a good testament to my basic teaching: Wake Up and STOP instead of Wake Up and GO!

---

[1] *nccam.nih.gov/health/stress/relaxation.htm*, accessed 2/1/13.

[2] *www.mayoclinic.com/health/relaxation-technique/SR00007*, accessed 2/1/13.

[3] *web.mit.edu/newsoffice/2011/meditation-0505.html*, accessed 2/1/13.

[4] Dr. John L. Craven, "Meditation and Psychotherapy," *Canadian Journal of Psychiatry*, 34 (October 1989): 648–53.

[5] *www.dukehealth.org/health_library/health_articles/breathandbeing*, accessed 2/1/13.

Enjoying the Benefits of Meditation

When we meditate regularly using a technique that feels comfortable, we will begin to notice an inward transformation that carries with it many beneficial effects that can be felt throughout the day. We will know that our meditation "worked" when we see it playing out in our everyday lives. We begin living a life that we have always wanted to live. A regular meditation practice helps us to do the following:

- Improve concentration
- Deepen relaxation and relieve stress
- Slow breathing
- Widen our perspective
- Stay more centered in the moment throughout the day
- Calm our mind and reduce mental chatter
- Strengthen our ability to let things go
- Increase awareness of our thoughts, allowing us to reduce the effects of the negative ones
- Ease feelings of restlessness
- Tap into our innermost self
- Cultivate a deep knowing that we are all connected, that all life is one

Parting Thoughts

Meditation helps us calm our minds so that we can go within and hear the "whisperings of our hearts." Starting our day in stillness helps us connect with our inner guidance and center of peace. Through our morning meditation, we bring our heart, mind, and body into alignment with the intention of greeting the moments of our day centered and grounded in who we are. This allows us to be more present and mindful as we go about our lives, bringing more opportunities for happiness. We are human beings, of course, so we need little reminders to stay the course as much as possible. That is where the next step in The Practice comes in: Living Present.

Takeaway Seeds

SEED 1 Each day is a gift.

SEED 2 Morning meditation helps us go inward and tap into the place that calms, centers, and empowers us.

SEED 3 Meditation practice is all about the practice, not the result.

SEED 4 Life is completely unpredictable. We can plan and do our very best, but in the end we have no control over the outcome.

SEED 5 The peace and mindfulness gained from having meditated shows up in our daily lives when we are patient instead of anxious, loving instead of unkind, and compassionate instead of judgmental.

CHAPTER 2

LIVING PRESENT

Carrying Our Inner Peace
Throughout the Day

*"You must live in the present,
launch yourself on every wave, find
your eternity in each moment."*

—Henry David Thoreau

Many great teachers today talk about living in the present moment. Of them, two of my favorites are Thich Nhat Hanh and Eckhart Tolle. Thanks to "Thay"—as Thich Nhat Hanh's students refer to him—mindfulness has become a mainstream concept, and Eckhart Tolle has made this practice accessible to millions of people through *The Power of Now*. I owe these teachers a big "thank you" for Living Present!

Living Present is being mindful of each moment of our day—no matter how ordinary it may seem. In my workshops, I always say, "When Living Present, we are aware of the ordinary moments of our lives, which are extraordinary." When we are mindful, we are "showing up" for life, fully aware of the present moment and its potential gifts. With yesterday's worries and tomorrow's concerns pulling our attention in two different directions, it is easy to fall out of alignment. All too often, we live in yesterday's happiness and become upset that it is not happening today. When we fall prey to the tugs of the mind, we miss out on the extraordinary, which is available to us in every moment.

The practice of Living Present helps us to remember that we only have right now. This day is a gift. Keeping this in mind helps us to stay centered and find our balance so that we can respond to the events of the day from a place of strength and compassion. This is the source of peace we tapped into during our Waking Up Meditation, and it is what we want to carry with us throughout our day.

In this chapter, we will discuss the three components of Living Present: the Sacred Mantra, Focused Attention, and Reading for Inspiration. But before we discuss the specifics of how to apply each of these to our day, let us look at what it is that keeps us from Living Present in the first place—the mind.

THE NATURE OF THE MIND

"The happiness of your life depends upon the quality of your thoughts; therefore, guard accordingly and take care that you entertain no notions unsuitable to virtue and reasonable nature."

—Marcus Aurelius

These are strong words from Marcus Aurelius: "The happiness of your life depends upon the quality of your thoughts." Remember how I started the preface with Abraham Lincoln's words: "People are just as happy as they make up their minds to be"? The mind is so crucial to living a happy life that we must take a close look at it. We think a lot, don't we? We think about the past, and we think about the future. Sometimes we even think about thinking! It seems our minds constantly want to be engaged. It is the nature of the mind to think, analyze, critique, and make sense of everything we perceive. So why is that a problem? Aurelius and Lincoln are saying that it is our biggest problem, our greatest obstacle—our happiness depends on it. This is really big.

Let me ask you: Have you ever tried to *not* think about something, but your mind just keeps harping on the same old thing and will not listen to you when you tell it to stop? We have all experienced this in some capacity—like the curious phenomenon of getting a song stuck in our heads, maybe even one we do not really like. It goes on and on like a broken record. Not only can we not turn it off, we cannot even turn down the volume. And that is not the worst part of it. Our mind is not just stuck on one thing, on a song. It is thinking about *everything*!

We wonder why we are feeling so tired and drained and why we often do not feel good about ourselves. This is the work of the mind. It jumps around from random thought to thought, rarely making any sense or giving us a break, let alone peace of mind. Take a look at the following illustration of the mind.

When we take a moment to look at our thoughts, we realize just how unruly our minds are. It seems our thoughts are in charge, and we are just along for the ride. If we were in control, we would think happy, uplifting thoughts, not stressful, depressing thoughts. Right? So how do we become aware of the dialogue that is going on in there and take back control? After all, our happiness depends on it. We do this by becoming more aware of our thoughts.

When we first begin a practice that is meant to calm the mind and bring us inner peace, we very quickly see that we have a huge problem. We really had not realized how active our mind has been, and trying to get it to quiet down can seem impossible. Little by little, we start becoming aware and begin to really hear what our mind has been saying to us. We discover that these random thoughts are going on all the time, and they are usually rooted in the past or the future. The majority of them dwell on the negative, highlighting our fears, shortcomings, and failures—and not only our own, but other people's as well. Living in the past and future along with any negativity attached to thoughts is draining and exhausting. Thinking like this takes a lot of energy.

The mind is talking, talking, talking . . . and we are listening, listening, listening. The voice never stops judging or gossiping; it judges what we do and what we think. It tells us what is right and what is wrong, and what is ugly and what is beautiful.

When I began paying attention to my thoughts, I discovered that I was trying to think my way through everything. I truly believed that if I concentrated long enough, I could solve and handle whatever was going on in my life. Sadly, I identified so much with my thoughts that I believed they were who I was: *I am my thoughts.* If a thought said, *Don't go to the movie tonight with your friends because they don't like*

you—call and tell them you are not feeling well, I believed it
and canceled. Before treatment, in my early days, if a thought
said, *You are too fat, so vomit after eating lunch,* I believed it
even though I was five-feet-six and weighed 125 pounds! I
was living in my mind.

Most of us live the life our thoughts are telling us to live,
and whether they are true or not, we obey. When we see this
visual of our mind, we can take a pause and ask ourselves,
Could it be that my thoughts are the problem? I find that the
answer is often a resounding yes!

Through my personal experience, I have come across a
piece of good news: we can change this way of thinking with
practice and consistent work. The mind *can* be trained. We
can take back our control, live in the present moment, and
"be as happy as we make up our minds to be."

I am really not sure why the mind is constantly going, but
after years of observing and studying the mind, I have come
to understand that this seems to be its job. When we become
awakened to this truth, the hold the mind has on us starts
to loosen. We are not so upset by its chatter. We question
what it says to us and do not blindly believe the monologue.
Little by little, we start to have a separation, a detachment.
We become the "witness" of our mind as it thinks all these

random thoughts, and gently we begin the work of keeping it focused on what matters most: positive qualities such as love, peace, truth, compassion, patience, and gratitude. We are able to keep it focused on the things we really do *need* to think about by choosing *what* we are going to think about and *when* we are going to think about it. This is the training.

On a retreat in 2008, my friend, the medical intuitive Caroline Myss, beautifully stated, "The soul always knows what to do to heal itself. The challenge is to silence the mind." This is what we do every morning in our meditation; we are letting our souls heal us as we silence the mind by allowing the thoughts to come and go. We now become the one in charge of our minds and, as a result, our lives.

Short of reaching a state of enlightenment, I do not believe we are ever going to change the nature of the mind. It is always going to throw something at us from time to time. One day recently, as I was going about my usual routines, my mind said, *You do not measure up and will not be okay at the luncheon today.*

I stopped dead in my tracks and said to myself, *What?*

I could hear my heart pounding, and then I immediately started silently repeating my Sacred Mantra, which I will introduce to you in the next section. My heart calmed down, and I then said to myself, *Of course I will be okay at the luncheon! I cannot wait to see my friends and they me.*

In the earlier days of my life, I believed I did not measure up and was not good enough. So back then, when a thought like that came to me, I doubted myself and ended up feeling "less than." Today, after training my mind with the use of my Sacred Mantra, I know I am worthy, and I can let these negative thoughts go and return to the present moment "without another thought." Let us turn our attention now to the Sacred Mantra so that you can truly understand what a wonderful tool this practice can be in your life.

THE SACRED MANTRA

"Stop the flow of your words. Open the window of your heart . . . and let the spirit speak."

—Rumi

The Sacred Mantra is "the way the mind finds the heart," as described in the marvelous book *The Way of a Pilgrim* by R.M. French. This is just so beautifully stated and a great way for me to introduce the Sacred Mantra to you. Generally speaking, in The Practice, the Sacred Mantra is a word, phrase, verse, or prayer with a long history of use that is hallowed or considered holy by the tradition or culture from which it originated, which you have personally chosen for your use.

Why do I call it a *Sacred* Mantra? The word *sacred* is broadly defined by social scientists as that which is set apart from the ordinary and worthy of veneration. So what makes the mantra sacred is its intimate association with saints, mystics, or other spiritual masters, teachers, and traditions. Sir Isaac Newton said, "If I have been able to see farther, it was only because I have stood on the shoulders of giants." This is what we are doing when we use our Sacred Mantra: we are standing on the shoulders of these magnificent giants.

The word *mantra* (sometimes spelled and pronounced *mantram*) is a Sanskrit word that, according to a definition from a teacher in one of my yoga classes, means "mind travel". He says that "a mantra traverses the mind and sends us into another space." When I hear an analogy that speaks to me so directly, like this one, I breathe out a smile! This definition resonates with me because it is so simple to visualize and understand and has no religious meaning associated with it. For example, in the anecdote I shared about when my mind told me I was not going to be okay at the luncheon, my Sacred Mantra sent my mind into another space—a space where I knew I was okay and where I am loved and I love my life.

In *The Yoga Sutras of Patanjali*, Sri Swami Satchidananda comments, "The meaning of *mantram* is 'that which keeps the mind steady and produces the proper effect.'" I experience this steadiness of mind and its benefit every time I use my Sacred Mantra. I love sharing this with anyone who is interested because its power is amazing and incredibly transformative.

Simply put, to use your Sacred Mantra means to silently repeat it to yourself under any number of circumstances throughout the day. It intercepts or slows down the rush of thoughts, helping you to act mindfully rather than to mindlessly react. Unlike an affirmation, a Sacred Mantra is not a saying we use to motivate or empower ourselves. A mantra is sacred because when we use it, we are calling upon the strength of all the great saints, masters, and traditions that have used it before us for support, spiritual well-being, and deep connection.

This idea that we can gain strength from those who came before us is aptly illustrated by the words Rosa Parks used to describe what gave her strength the day she refused to give up her seat on a Montgomery, Alabama, bus in 1955. She said, "I knew that I had the strength of my ancestors behind me." Each time I hear these words and visualize Rosa

Parks on the bus that day with her unwavering strength and bravery, tears come to my eyes. This is what a Sacred Mantra offers. It is not only there to remind you that you are supported, but it also allows you to tap into the love, energy, power, and strength of those who have used it for the very same purpose.

The Buddhist mantra *Om mani padme hum,* for example, has been used by millions of people around the world for centuries. When I close my eyes and say that particular mantra, I can feel those millions of people together with the Buddha connecting with what they call the "precious jewel within the lotus"—the heart.

In the middle of writing this book I went on a retreat. At this retreat were offerings of bodywork, so I scheduled an "integrated energy work" session. When I arrived at my appointment, the therapist asked me if I had ever had anything like this done before. I told her I had not, and she explained how this energy work is performed with specific hand positions around the body while the receiver is fully clothed to gently clear energy blocks that have accumulated from physical, mental, emotional, or spiritual trauma. I thought to myself, *Whoa, I have had all of these, so I sure picked the right treatment for me!*

As I lay on the table, I began breathing deeply and repeated my Sacred Mantra throughout the ninety-minute session, which went by in a flash. When she was finished, we talked. She explained that it was normal for some emotions or thoughts to come up over the next twenty-four hours and that I should drink lots of water. As I sat and listened to the therapist, I felt incredibly peaceful and present. I had a deep sense that all was well with my life. Then she asked if she could share something that came up during the treatment, to which I replied, "Of course."

She proceeded to explain that the neck area represents our support system. Through her work, she could often sense the strength of this support—some weak and some strong. In my case, she said, "I have never in all my years sensed what you have—I sensed a very long and ancient support system from your ancestors." She told me she really did not understand what this meant specifically in terms of my life and asked if I knew what she was talking about. I smiled so big, and goose bumps popped out on my arms. I felt such incredible warmth in my heart as I responded, "Yes, I know exactly what it is and who they are."

I left that treatment with an affirmation of what I had already known: the ancestors, saints, and mystics connected with the repetition of my Sacred Mantra were supporting me, always. These words of Native American writer Linda Hogan came to life for me that day: "Walking, I am listening to a deeper way. Suddenly all my ancestors are behind me. Be still, they say. Watch and listen. You are the result of the love of thousands." I am loved.

WHAT THE SACRED MANTRA DOES. The mantra is a "thought interceptor"—a word or phrase that intercepts stressful, negative, or repetitive thoughts, mostly in the past and future, and carries us into a calmer, more grounded place in the present. The Sacred Mantra helps us to traverse the mind so that we can access the space of stillness among the random thoughts in our mind.

Let me share with you another personal example: Several months ago, I went for my yearly mammogram. As I waited for the results, the nurse came in and said the doctor wanted to speak with me. A rush of thoughts entered my mind: *What could be wrong?* But instead of letting those thoughts continue and allowing my mind to go into a dark and negative place, I started repeating my Sacred Mantra—*My God and My All*—as I walked into the doctor's office. I was able to be in the moment and listen, really listen, to what she had to say instead of feeling scared and distracted by the worries. I was calm and present with my doctor. She said she had seen something suspicious, nothing too alarming, but she wanted to be certain and asked me to stay for an ultrasound.

I agreed, of course, and continued to repeat my Sacred Mantra the entire time—during the test and while waiting for the results. When she called me in to say that everything was fine, I breathed a sigh of relief and left her office. While my Sacred Mantra did not make the test results fine, it made *me* feel fine, fully in the present moment, able to accept any news I might receive.

Eckhart Tolle says, "Be present as the watcher of your mind—of your thoughts and emotions as well as your reactions in various situations." My Sacred Mantra was the tool that helped me be present as the "watcher" of my mind. This power of the Sacred Mantra connects us deep within, where love and strength reside. When we repeat our Sacred Mantra, we connect inwardly with who we are, with that great source of strength inside us—the Lord, Source, God, the Light, Beloved, Divine Guide—whatever we choose to call it.

In this way, the mantra is our support and strength, helping us handle anything that life sends our way. Remember, the Sacred Mantra does not take away all the things that life has in store for us. Instead, it stops the rush of the negative or stressful thoughts so we can be present to our life in the moment and make decisions and take action from a place of awareness, love, compassion, and strength.

When our thoughts begin to wander, usually to the past or future, repeating our Sacred Mantra brings us right back to the present, allowing us to be more mindful and more aware of what is going on around us at that moment. For example, if I notice that my mind is wandering while I am having a conversation with my husband, I can repeat my Sacred Mantra and immediately return my full attention to him. In this way, we really begin to "be" with everyone and everything in our lives because we are practicing Living Present. We are showing up for our life! The Sacred Mantra is an important and helpful tool when practicing Focused Attention, which is discussed later in this chapter.

Someone once asked me how I can repeat my mantra and still be present to the conversation I am having. "Isn't the Sacred Mantra keeping us from being present to the person?" she asked me. This is a very good question. Here is what I know to be true: In the early days of my life, I rarely talked to a person without my mind commenting on what he or she was saying, thinking about what I needed to do later in the day, or wondering what I was going to say once it was my turn to speak. You may be able to relate to this. Since it is the nature of the mind to think, it naturally does this even during conversations. However, now that I have The Practice, I am training my mind to be present and quiet when I am having a conversation with someone so that I can give that person my full attention. The Sacred Mantra is the tool that brings my mind back to the moment, back to the conversation at hand. As a result, I have become a great listener, which has enriched my life beautifully.

Sometimes during stressful, difficult, or uncomfortable conversations, I may have to repeat my Sacred Mantra several times, but always with the intention of being a more present listener. When we use our mantra to intercept critical or angry reactions, we are strengthening an important muscle that gives us greater control over how we will choose to respond to people and in situations. Instead of living our lives reacting to people, places, and things, we are able to choose an action from a place of calmness and thoughtfulness. Viktor Frankl, the author of the must-read book *Man's Search for Meaning*, says, "Between stimulus and response, there is a space. In that space lies our freedom and our power to choose our response. In our response lies our growth and our happiness."

Here is that word *happiness* again! Not only is Frankl talking about happiness, he is also talking about freedom. When we are at the mercy of our negative, angry thoughts, we most likely will react with anger. That is stimulus and response. But if we can immediately start repeating our Sacred Mantra when these stressful thoughts begin, we create space. In that space, we have the opportunity to choose our action; this is living in freedom. We are not at the mercy of anything or anyone, especially not our thoughts; we are light, happy, and free.

Likewise, our Sacred Mantra is incredibly supportive when we are feeling stressed, under a lot of pressure, frightened, or in danger. Repeating our Sacred Mantra in these situations brings us into the present moment, where we can be alert, calm, and steady so that we are able to deal with whatever threat is in front of us. In times of great stress, when outside influences are completely beyond our control, the Sacred Mantra connects us deep within, providing us with comfort, giving us a gentle hug, and helping us to accept what is and to rest in that quiet place within, where we know all is well.

SELECTING A SACRED MANTRA. There are thousands of mantras, sacred verses, and prayer words in every tradition. You may already have a specific prayer or mantra that you use in your life. If it works for you, and it comes from a great master, saint, mystic, or tradition, stick with it. If you do not have one, take your time selecting it. To begin, there is a list of some suggested Sacred Mantras in Appendix A. If you do not see one that appeals to you right away, choose one for a day or a week and use it consistently. You will know if it feels comfortable and resonates with you after some use. If not, move on to another one and continue this process until you find one that really speaks to you and you feel as if you can live with it for the rest of your life.

Once you select a Sacred Mantra, the idea is not to change it. See "The Staff of Life," a sidebar that follows this section, for a brief explanation. My Sacred Mantra, *My God and My All*, is a holy phrase spoken by Saint Francis of Assisi, whom I started loving as a child. He spoke deeply to my heart with his love for animals (and for all life) and talked often of how to find peace. So when it came time to choose my Sacred Mantra, I chose this one. And now, after decades of practice and repetition, I feel as if I am walking with Saint Francis and that he is giving me strength, love, and companionship.

If you do not see a Sacred Mantra on the list, you can seek out a Sacred Mantra by doing your own reading of sacred texts. The only guideline here is that you do not make up your Sacred Mantra. As I said earlier, it is not the same thing as an affirmation. Remember, what makes a mantra sacred is its long history of use by the great masters, mystics, and saints (as well as by people just like us). It allows us to tap into the power of those who have followed this path before us.

In your search for a mantra, keep looking for one that you feel drawn to. Choose one that feels comfortable, that resonates with you on a deep level, and that touches your heart. Being able to pronounce your Sacred Mantra is important. I have a friend who chose a mantra because she loved its meaning, but because she had trouble pronouncing the words, it became an impediment. She ended up changing it. I also recommend not choosing one that offends you in any way or does not feel quite right for whatever reason. If you settle for a word or phrase that sounds good but does not feel right, you may have a problem integrating it into your life.

Some Sacred Mantras will be just a couple of words, a few phrases, or even a few sentences. The length does not make one better than another. But if you choose one of the longer ones and need it in a pinch, you can shorten it. Whatever Sacred Mantra you choose, be sure it leaves you with a heartfelt feeling when you say it. It is with you for the rest of your life!

The Staff of Life

Gandhi said, "The mantram becomes one's Staff of Life and carries one through every ordeal. Each repetition has a new meaning, carrying you nearer and nearer to God." In other words, the mantra becomes a necessity that helps us cope with those things in life that are trying, stressful, and difficult. The more we use it, the more support it gives us by helping us tap into our inner source of strength and love.

Although many people are not quite sure about committing themselves to just one mantra for the rest of their lives, those people who have used their Sacred Mantra consistently for many decades, as I have, can attest to the fact that it truly does become a "Staff of Life," a valued friend and companion who is always with us, especially during the most troubling times of our lives. This idea of using only one mantra can be illustrated here and has ancient roots. Patanjali wrote (as translated by Sri Swami Satchidananda), "The practice of concentration on a single subject is the best way to prevent the obstacles and their accompaniments."

He comments further on this sutra (precept): "The point here is that we should not keep changing our object of concentration. When you decide on one thing, stick to it whatever happens. There is no value in digging shallow wells in a hundred places. Decide on one place and dig deep." Many masters who came after Patanjali also espoused this tenet. And I am happy to say I have been sticking with my Sacred Mantra for over seventeen years quite simply because it works!

When choosing a Sacred Mantra, some people may be concerned they might not pick the "best" one. But no mantra is better than another. In essence, they are all one. They all take us to the same place within and support us in the same way, giving us exactly what we need in the moment. What we need may take different forms and perhaps even come to us in different words or prayers, but it is the mantra itself that is caring for us and lovingly guiding us through our difficulties.

When Gandhi was assassinated on January 30, 1948, his last words were "Rama, Rama." His mantra journeyed with him up until the moment of his death—never leaving his side. Likewise, after an assassination attempt was made on Pope John Paul II in 1981, I heard that he also turned to his sacred phrase, "Oh Maria Madre Mia." While the pope may not have referred to these words as his Sacred Mantra, this phrase seemed to serve the same purpose. These great masters are an inspiration for our own spiritual journey, and I encourage you to give this tool in The Practice a chance before deciding you could never live with just one mantra.

WHEN AND HOW TO USE THE SACRED MANTRA.

The Sacred Mantra can and should be used anytime, day or night, whenever you want or need it. In the beginning, use it whenever you think about it, no matter what you are doing, to get your mind accustomed to the activity. The Hindu tradition says mantra repetition is the "easiest practice" because you do not need to go to a particular place or set aside a particular time such as you would for meditation. In other words, you do not need anything outside you; it is always within. Wherever you are, wherever you go, your Sacred Mantra is always with you. My mantra is my friend, my Beloved, always in my heart. All I need to do is call upon it and repeat it as often as possible.

It may seem very mechanical at first, and you may ask yourself, *Why am I repeating this?* Do not bother about the why or the automatic feeling you have in the beginning; just keep repeating it, and you will soon see that it becomes a habit, and its deep meaning will have opened up within your heart. You will soon discover how wonderful it is to repeat your Sacred Mantra in the most mundane of places, such as when you are waiting in line at the grocery store and you start feeling agitated because the cashier or customer is taking too long, or when something on the news gets you riled up. In both of these cases and in more disturbing situations, the Sacred Mantra serves to calm those agitated, stressful feelings by bringing you back to a centered place, the present moment.

Many have asked me, "Do we really just start repeating these words in our head in line at the grocery store?" And I always smile and say, "Yes. It is so much better than getting agitated and annoyed, causing our day to be full of stress." I promise that after a time of using the Sacred Mantra, something incredible starts to shift; it no longer feels awkward or mechanical. It feels calming and comforting.

I used to love using my Sacred Mantra while waiting in the car for my daughter's after-school pickup. It helped me to have patience if she was running late, and it released my expectation that we should hurry up and move on to the next activity of the day. Most important, it helped me to be present to her at the end of her long school day.

The repetition of the Sacred Mantra is really magical when coupled with any form of exercise. When using it this way, you connect to that deep source of energy within you. Some of my friends use it during walking, swimming, or jogging to help boost their energy or increase their endurance. A good friend of mine told me she uses it during her tennis matches;

it helps her stay focused, in the present, and "in the zone." I use my Sacred Mantra during my walks after my morning meditation and during my yoga practice—I simply love it!

Many people use their Sacred Mantra in situations where they just want to remind themselves to be more open and receptive to life. Others use it just before beginning a new activity or as a way to transition to the next event in the day, to set a positive intention or to check within for strength. A close friend of mine uses it before answering the telephone to make sure she is centered and present for the caller. All of these are great ways to incorporate the Sacred Mantra into your day.

The Sacred Mantra is also used after the Reflection exercise, the last part of The Practice, which closes out the day. (Reflection is discussed in Chapter 3.) It is a beautiful way to drift off to sleep, keeping your mind clear and peaceful. Also, you may wish to repeat your mantra before or during your morning meditation and as you leave your meditation space. Coupling your Sacred Mantra with your meditation practice as you leave your space keeps that energy of peacefulness with you as you begin your daily activities.

Have some fun and experiment using your Sacred Mantra during the typical activities of your day. For example, what is your mind doing when you are brushing your teeth? What about when you are in the shower? Someone once said, "I do my best thinking in the shower!" That may be true, so next time you are in the shower, pay attention to what your mind is saying. If it is just ruminating about what happened yesterday or listing all the things you need to do today and making you feel stressed, insert your Sacred Mantra into that stream of thought and watch the transformation that follows.

Another way I love to use my Sacred Mantra is to write it down. This has been a wonderful source of support and joy for me for many years. When I use the word *support* here, I literally mean that writing my Sacred Mantra kept me from worrying myself silly when my daughter went off to college. The thought of her going away to that great unknown was mentally very stressful for me. She and I are very close, and somehow I felt that even though I knew she was completely ready to be on her own, I had a false sense that I somehow had control when she was living at home. But now that she was going away, everything would be completely out of my control.

I knew immediately that I wanted to stay loving, grounded, and supportive, but at the same time I was very worried. I bought many small notebooks and put her name, Michelle, at the top of the page and started writing, *My God and My All,* over and over again until the book was filled. My intention was to calm my mind and intercept this worry with a sense of well-being and, at the same time, to send this precious Sacred Mantra to Michelle. I continued to write my Sacred Mantra for Michelle during her entire four years of college. It is truly amazing that when I write my mantra with intention and concentration, a sense of love and well-being immediately washes over my entire body.

Admittedly, this act of writing the Sacred Mantra over and over again may sound a little strange, but believe me, I did not make it up. Many have engaged in this practice. For example, in the Foreword of the book *In Quest of God* by Swami Ramdas, spiritual teacher Ram Dass (also known as Richard Alpert) writes of a "diary" left behind by his guru, Neem Karoli Baba, following his death. Ram Dass says, "I was told he kept a 'diary.' I was most curious as to what such an enlightened being would find worthy of committing to paper. When I was finally shown the exercise books which served as his diary, I found page after page, book after book, in his Hindi script, of the name RAM, repeated again and again." So when we use our Sacred Mantra this way, we are in good company!

This writing has become a beautiful practice for me that I do every day. Some days I write it for loved ones, for world crises and tragedies like the Newtown shootings, or for myself. Each time, I write with the intention to send love, peace, and wellness to the person or situation. I recommend it greatly. You may enjoy and find this activity meaningful as well. Read about Sacred Mantra writing and artwork in chapter 4, and try it for yourself.

As you can now see, I can absolutely attest that you will find that the longer you use your Sacred Mantra, the more it comes to you unbidden. In the Foreword of *The Way of a Pilgrim,* Huston Smith explains this beautifully: "One who accustoms himself to this appeal experiences as a result so deep a consolation and so great a need to offer the prayer always that he can no longer live without it, and it will begin to voice itself within him of its own accord."

If you are anxious and afraid, your Sacred Mantra may come to you to remind you of your source of strength and courage. At times, my Sacred Mantra actually feels as if it is giving me a comforting hug. Your Sacred Mantra may even come to you during times of joy and celebration. In 2008, at my daughter's college graduation, my Sacred Mantra began playing in my mind, and I remember thinking how unbelievably wonderful it felt. It was the first time it had come so loudly and joyfully while I was in a great state of happiness.

After years of practice, it is such a gift when your Sacred Mantra plays in the background of your mind. What would your mind be doing otherwise? Sometimes, we need a reminder, so take another look at the illustration on page 59. Most likely it would be worrying about something in the future or ruminating about something from the past. When your Sacred Mantra becomes such a part of you that you turn to it without too much forethought (or none at all), you realize that you are taking back control of your mind and your life.

Poet Mary Oliver asks us, "Tell me, what is it you plan to do with your one wild and precious life?" By taking back control of our mind, we take control of our lives and then we are truly able to live the incredible life we are meant to have.

WHAT IS AN AFFIRMATION?

People ask me regularly during my workshops how the Sacred Mantra differs from an affirmation. I answer in this way: Everything I know about affirmations I learned from Louise Hay in 1986, whom I lovingly refer to as the "queen" of affirmations. Her first book, *Heal Your Body*, which was published in 1976, was one of the earliest Western books to tackle the mind-body connection. I find Louise a true inspiration for living an amazing life. An affirmation is a positive statement or judgment declared to be true that is intended to provide assurance in the face of fear, doubt, stress, and worry. These statements, either spoken aloud or said silently, are meant to replace negative thoughts in the mind with positive ones.

Affirmations can be beneficial and have a wonderful place in The Practice—after meditation, before going to sleep, and throughout the day whenever you need one and as a complement to your Sacred Mantra. With all the negative chatter going on in the mind, sometimes an affirmation is exactly what is needed to get the mind to change course. In order to calm down, the mind might want that added verbal assurance that everything really is fine. For example, if I am in a stressful situation and my mind is starting down a negative path, I may use the affirmation "Barb, you are strong and capable; all is well," and then follow with my Sacred Mantra.

THE VALUE OF THE SACRED MANTRA. The value of the Sacred Mantra is easy to see as early as the first time you use it to stop an unwanted thought. When you intercept the thought, a noticeable shift in your frame of mind happens almost immediately; the negative thinking comes to a stop for that moment and you have an immediate opportunity to get around that obstacle. With the Sacred Mantra, you can instantly reach a calmer state. A negative thought and a positive thought cannot exist in the mind at the same time. So the more you use the Sacred Mantra when your mind starts down that negative, stressful path, the more often you will be in a present positive state of mind.

It takes practice to fully incorporate the use of the Sacred Mantra into your life, but you do not have to wait until you have hours of practice to notice a shift and experience the benefits listed at the end of this section. For example, when I am having negative thoughts, and I intercept them with the repetition of my Sacred Mantra, it stops the negative thoughts instantly because I am actually taking another route. I am shifting my thinking process to another direction. This is not to say that I will not encounter those obstacles again, but when I do, I simply continue to train my mind not to dwell there by repeating my Sacred Mantra. Here is a beautiful commentary by Sri Swami Satchidananda in *The Yoga Sutras of Patanjali* on the topic of mantra repetition:

> You get in tune with the cosmic power. By that tuning you feel that force in you, imbibe all those qualities, get the cosmic vision, transcend all your limitations, and finally become that

transcendental reality. Normally, the mind and body limit you, but by holding something infinite you slowly raise yourself from the finite objects that bind you and transcend them. Through that you get rid of all the obstacles and your path is made easy.

The Sacred Mantra is "something infinite," and by using it, the value becomes especially apparent when we are faced with extraordinary or upsetting events. There are times we will have been wronged or treated unfairly or something terrible will have happened. How would we like to handle these situations? Since you are reading this book, you would probably choose to respond as lovingly, compassionately, and calmly as you can. The Sacred Mantra is not going to make the situation go away or change what has occurred, but it will allow you to tap into your inner source of strength, as Sri Swami Satchidananda said, "by that tuning you feel that force in you" to help you make sound, thoughtful choices and take appropriate actions that will deliver the best possible outcome.

When we are faced with something we are not sure about or that we simply do not understand, we are going to get worried, feel stressed, and maybe even be scared. That is okay. It is normal. The point here is this: Worry is part of our human existence. The Sacred Mantra is not going to make us never worry again. Rather, because worry often comes in tandem with negative emotions, the idea is to acknowledge the worry we are feeling, then ask ourselves, *Is there something we can do about the worry?* If there is, we can move forward by taking the appropriate action.

This may be as simple as breathing and then doing whatever needs to be done in the moment. If it is a worry we cannot do anything about, then the action to take is to stop our mind from ruminating or obsessing about it. This can be easier said than done! By repeating our Sacred Mantra, we give ourselves the much-needed space between the worrisome thoughts to consider what action we are called to take and then take it.

Again, the truth is this: If continuing to worry and obsess could actually change the outcome, then I would say we should keep worrying. But we all have firsthand experience that worry just simply does not work. Worrying magnifies our concerns and increases our stress level. As Gabrielle Bernstein says in her lectures and in her book *Add More Ing to Your Life: A Hip Guide to Happiness,* "Worry is a prayer to chaos." So we must find a better way if it is happiness we truly seek. The Sacred Mantra is the better way!

Additionally, many times when we are at a loss about how we can help others who have suffered or are suffering from some tragedy or wrongdoing, repeating our Sacred Mantra specifically for those people allows us to send loving and healing energy their way. How many times have we all said, "I wish there were something I could do for the victims and families of a tragedy"? Repeating our Sacred Mantra for them is a big something we can all do.

The Sacred Mantra Shift

One day toward the end of my mother's life, when she was very ill, I had to run to the grocery store to get her some things she needed. I lived just a mile away, and even though I did not want to leave her, I knew I could get back quickly. I rushed through the store and got back to my car in record time, but instead of walking the cart back to the front of the store as I usually do, I left it in the lot.

As I started to pull out of my parking space, I heard someone shouting at me: "How lazy are you? What's the matter with you? Put that cart away!"

Outwardly I ignored the person, but inside, my heart started racing. *Why is he yelling at me?* I thought. He doesn't know what is going on in my life or why I am in such a rush. If he did know, he would feel terrible! And then I started to get angry with him. My Sacred Mantra started going—in fact, I had a double track going!

In this convergence of Sacred Mantra and anger and feeling bad that I had "done something wrong," an amazing transformation happened. I thought to myself about how often I had judged somebody, mostly silently, for doing something similar, for something that seemed, from my point of view, selfish or thoughtless. I acknowledged to myself that we rarely know the whole story from another person's point of view. In that moment, I saw the complete story of judgment—how we get our own thoughts going about things without ever knowing the truth. The words my mother said regularly in my life came to me: "You never know another person's life without walking in their shoes."

In that situation, I became free of judgment. Today, when my mind starts to make a judgment, my Sacred Mantra comes immediately, and I say to myself, "Barb, you have no idea what the story is here," and the judgment disappears. Sri Swami Satchidananda's words became a reality for me, and they can for you, too: "By holding something infinite you slowly raise yourself from the finite objects that bind you and transcend them. Through that, you get rid of all the obstacles and your path is made easy."

Enjoying the Benefits of a Sacred Mantra

When we intercept disquieting thoughts by repeating our mantra, prayer, or hallowed verse; when we turn to it for support, comfort, and strength; and even when it comes to us in times of joy, the benefits are many. Our Sacred Mantra helps us to do the following:

- Refocus our attention on the present moment
- Reduce stress and anxiety
- Quiet mental chatter and slow the speed of thoughts
- Ease negative emotions
- Manage stress and put it in perspective
- Soothe our nervous energy
- Access the "space between thoughts" to gain clarity
- Facilitate personal transformation
- Connect us to our deep spiritual source
- Be the person we want to be and to live the life we want to live
- Cultivate compassion, love, and forgiveness
- See others as members of our own family and recognize that we are all one

FOCUSED ATTENTION

"The moments of our daily life may appear commonplace, but they carry enormous significance. When we look upon every moment as sacred, a new energy flows into our lives."

—Vinoba Bhave

On the surface, our daily lives might seem ordinary. Occasionally we attend a special event or something exciting happens, but for the most part, when we are not living mindfully in the present moment, we sort of just do what needs to be done and grab moments of enjoyment whenever we can. We might even think that much of what we do during the day is a waste of time or just a means to an end: *Let me get through these eight hours of work so that I can go home and watch my favorite television show tonight,* or *Let me get through this month so that I can go on vacation,* or *Let me get through this year so that I can graduate,* and so on.

Recently, in a workshop, one of the participants told me that she wakes up in the morning and tries to make it to six o'clock so she can have a glass of wine and coast through to the end of the day and go to bed feeling like she made it. I replied, "We are not just meant to survive in life, we are meant to thrive!" When we live by trying to "survive," the hours, days, months, and even years fly by, and they are lost to us forever. We really did not make them count. We were not living in the moment. Our attention was everywhere else but on that precious moment called *now*. As I said to my new friend from the workshop, "Fortunately, we know it does not have to be this way; we are not meant to live this way, and you *can* live the magnificent life you wish to live."

Just how do we make the moments of every day count no matter how insignificant or stressful our activities may seem? We practice Focused Attention: the second part of Living Present. But what does this mean? "Attention" is the act or state of applying the mind to something. When our attention is divided, it means we are paying attention to more than one thing. This reduces our ability to really be present to whatever it is we are doing.

Unfortunately, without awareness, we do this all the time. It has become our second nature. Fortunately, our *first* nature is to be present to everyone and everything in the moment. Simply put, when our attention is focused, we are present to only what we are doing—we are honoring the moment by giving it our all. We experience the moment more fully, which gives us a greater sense of fulfillment, gratitude, and ease.

The Gift of Choice

Why do we want to live in the present? There are many reasons, but here's a big one: The present is the only opportunity we have to make the choices that define our lives. In the present moment, we have the gift of choice. We cannot choose in the future, and we cannot choose in the past. Neither exists. This gift of choice is only available to us in the moment.

Can you see why we really do not want to miss out on the opportunity to make choices in the ordinary moments of our day? This is our life. These choices, one by one, make us the people we are. When we choose wisely and mindfully, we are loving, compassionate, and confident. I often say, "Living Present, we are aware of the ordinary moments of our lives, which are extraordinary." Each moment, each choice, counts.

WHEN TO PRACTICE FOCUSED ATTENTION. Practice Focused Attention all the time, in every moment! When you start the day with a meditation practice (which is practicing Focused Attention, by the way), you are already setting this wonderful intention to be present to your life. When you begin to engage with the outside world, really focus on what you are doing each moment. Place your full attention on the people you are interacting with, on the task at hand, and on the situation you are in. Your Sacred Mantra is used throughout the day as a reminder to return yourself to the present moment when you notice that your attention is starting to go off in unwanted directions.

WHERE TO PRACTICE FOCUSED ATTENTION. Practice Focused Attention wherever you are, no matter what you are doing—in your home with family members, in the garden, on walks, at work, at the grocery store, at parties, in your place of worship, in group settings, at workshops . . . the list goes on and on! I have been on several retreats with the very special Buddhist nun Pema Chödrön. When she says, "This very moment is the perfect teacher," I believe she is letting us in on a little secret: when we live in the present moment, we are able to accept everything that happens to us as a teaching moment, which we may be able to look back on and ultimately call a blessing.

HOW TO PRACTICE FOCUSED ATTENTION. Practice Focused Attention by making a choice to be present to everyone and everything in your life—one task or person at a time. When your mind wanders from the task at hand or the person you are interacting with, silently repeat your Sacred Mantra a couple of times to bring you back to the moment. This is similar to what you do in meditation: when your mind wanders, you let the thoughts pass and focus your attention on the object.

Doing one thing at a time may sound easy, but it is difficult. The mind has a hard time doing just one thing because it has spent many, many years doing several things at once. We take pride in how efficient we are by getting a lot done in a short time. Society rewards us for doing several jobs at once, for multitasking. At first glance, it may seem as if we are getting a lot more done, but the truth is, we are doing more things less well. We all want more time. So, in the beginning, we may think that by doing several things at once, we are giving ourselves additional time, but in reality, it is impossible to sustain this pace.

Ultimately, we end up making mistakes, sometimes serious ones, and then we need to correct our mistakes. In some instances, we have done something in a rush, not realizing the harm it may cause us or those around us. In cases like that, we cannot always make it right. When we live this way, we end up not really living our lives; we feel resentful and end up wishing we had our precious time back.

Many of us, like me, who are in middle age think that our memories are "going bad." I say to myself, *Oh, I don't remember . . . I must be getting old!* But I have found that this is an excuse—a very poor one at that. How often have you met someone new, and then as soon as the person walks away, you forget his or her name? This used to happen to me all the time because instead of focusing my attention on the moment at hand and listening carefully, part of me was busy anticipating what I would say next. Now, with practice, I really focus on what the person is saying, and I then respond with whatever comes naturally. Today, I, more often than not, do recall the person's name.

I may be getting older, but my inability to remember what I went downstairs for really is not my age—it is a lack of Focused Attention. If I am walking down the stairs letting my mind think about the many other things it would love to think about, how could I possibly remember what it was I went downstairs for? But if I silently repeat my Sacred Mantra when I go down the stairs, I most certainly go straight to what I went down there for.

Let's look at some other ways to practice Focused Attention:

➤ When talking to someone, look the person in the eyes and do not let your mind wander. Remember, repeat your Sacred Mantra to bring your mind back to the person and the conversation.

🖎 When driving, give the road your full attention; turn off the radio and stay off the cell phone. (Oh my gosh, this sounds impossible!) Try it and discover how calm you feel once you reach your destination.

🖎 When watching TV, do not snack on food or drinks. Really pay attention to what is happening on the screen. If the program is not worth your full attention, maybe you are being called to do something else with your time.

🖎 When reading, leave the radio and television off; do not snack. Love the book you are reading and give it your full attention. If you cannot do this, maybe read something else.

🖎 When eating, really look at and taste your food; savor each bite. Put down the newspaper, turn off the TV, and stay off the cell phone until you are finished. You just may end up eating healthier food, eating less, and really enjoying your meal.

THE VALUE OF FOCUSED ATTENTION. The Buddha said, "As you walk and eat and travel, be where you are. Otherwise you will miss most of your life." Can you imagine missing out on your life—on your "one precious life," as Mary Oliver calls it? On retreats James Finley often says one of my favorite lines that goes straight to my heart every time: "If we are not careful, we will miss our own life."

Each of our lives is magnificent, and our world needs each of us—so the last thing we want to do is miss it. When we make a real effort to be more present in the moments of our lives, our awareness begins to expand: We notice more details, some big and some little, that somehow seem more significant and more alive to us, and we can actually start to see the impact of these details on our lives and on the lives of others. We may see blessings whereas before we were too overcome with worries or concerns or distractions to notice them.

Giving our family members and others our complete attention—really seeing them and hearing what they are saying—strengthens our relationships and deepens our personal connections. I love this beautiful line from the movie *Avatar:* "I see you." Living Present, we actually "see" all of life; we have a deep sense of being, of living.

By focusing our attention, we develop more patience in all situations, but especially in those where we are not in control and simply feel helpless. I have found that my lack of patience and stress come from not knowing all the details or not really being aware of what is going on around me. When we focus our attention on the present by repeating our Sacred Mantra, we gain awareness that provides us with a better understanding of the present circumstances, thereby giving us an opportunity to choose our action in any situation. The Sacred Mantra gives us the much-needed pause in situations to act instead of react.

How often have words crossed our lips that we wish we could take back? When we focus our attention and live in the present moment, we are much more likely to be patient and make wise choices. The following Arab proverb is a beautiful reminder for Living Present before we speak: "The words of the tongue should have three gatekeepers. Is it kind? Is it necessary? Is it true?"

When we practice Focused Attention, an incredible health benefit happens for us: our memory is improved. We are not bombarding the mind with unrelated bits of mostly random, useless information, so we are more efficient because our minds are not wandering or ruminating while we are trying to get something done. We end up having more energy because we are not so scattered. Believe it or not, when the mind is scattered, it takes a tremendous toll on both our mental and physical energy. The simple act of using our Sacred Mantra to bring us back to the present moment gives us the much-needed extra time, energy, and composure necessary for living our life with meaning and purpose.

Finding Life in the
Present Moment

"The mind can go in a thousand directions,
but on this beautiful path, I walk in peace.
With each step, a gentle wind blows.
With each step, a flower blooms."

—Thich Nhat Hanh

For a few years in the nineties, I studied under Thich Nhat Hanh, one of my most profound teachers. While attending my first retreat with him, he brilliantly described through word and action what it means to be mindful. Before meeting him, I was not sure what it meant to be mindful. He explained it with such deep beauty: "Life can only be found in the present moment."

When I heard these words, my heart opened. I said to myself, I want to be this way, to live this way. He then said, "The past is gone, the future is not yet here, and if we do not go back to ourselves in the present moment, we cannot be in touch with life."

My heart pounded loudly. *We cannot be in touch with life without going back to ourselves.* His words were like an arrow into my heart. *I have to find a way to get back to myself,* I thought. Although at the time I was not sure what it meant to "get back to myself," I had a deep desire to do it.

By the end of the weeklong silent retreat, after walking with this humble, beautiful master for an hour each day, I knew what mindfulness was, and I was in the present moment, in touch with my life.

Being in the presence of this holy man was one of the greatest experiences of my life. He exuded peace and was present to every single one of us in the group. As I watched and listened to him, it was clear that he was living every moment in the now and was completely in touch with his life. He emanated everything I thought our world should be: loving, peaceful, and compassionate. He embodied how I wanted to live my life—mindful and loving to everyone and everything, in the present moment. I credit my time with him for opening my heart to peace and to wanting love and peace for our world. The organization Peaceful Mind Peaceful Life is the result of this opening of my heart.

Enjoying the Benefits of Focused Attention

Although I often quote the Buddha, I am not a Buddhist. It is just that he is so darn practical when he says, "Do not dwell in the past, do not dream of the future, concentrate the mind on the present moment." And that is it—Live Present every ordinary moment of every day. You will discover for yourself that when you make the effort to be more aware of what is happening in the present moment, ordinary days are transformed into extraordinary days, and ordinary moments become sacred. Practicing Focused Attention helps us to do the following:

- Expand our awareness
- Increase our energy
- Improve our memory
- Create patience
- Eliminate stressful, negative thoughts
- Increase efficiency
- Encourage communication and deepen personal connections
- Reduce stress and improve health
- See our blessings

READING FOR INSPIRATION

*It takes a short amount of time
for information to get into the head;
but it can take a lifetime to get it
from the head to the heart.*

—Paraphrased from Eastern Orthodox Christianity

When I talk about Reading for Inspiration in my workshops—the third part of Living Present—I always get animated; I talk and talk and talk! For whatever reason, as a young girl, I never read. In fact, I am sorry to say this to all my wonderful teachers, but my sister actually read the books that were assigned to me in class and would even write the book reports. As a trade-off, I would do my sister's art assignments and some of her math. But for the past thirty years, reading has become an essential part of my life.

Just as the food we eat nourishes and strengthens the body, the books we read for inspiration nourish and enrich the mind. I thrive in my life and feed my soul with the reading I do daily. The books I recommend here as part of The Practice focus on the lives of the masters, mystics, saints, spiritual teachers, healers, and the great religions and spiritual traditions. You will notice that in almost every case, these books are written by the masters, saints, mystics, or teachers themselves. In general, these are not books written *about* them but *by* them.

As we read about the lives and experiences of these incredible human beings, in their own words, it slowly occurs to us that they really did not possess any extraordinary powers; they started out just like us. What makes them extraordinary is their deep desire and unwavering faith to live a life of love, purpose, and meaning. By example, they inspire us to uncover the Truth that we too are incredible human beings. Their words are a great comfort and support as we go within to find that deep source of love and strength, as they did.

When we read about the lives of these incredible men and women, it gives us great hope and strength to learn that we are not really any different from them. They did not have a preset program in their brains that said, "You are going to be enlightened; you are going to do many magnificent things in this world." They just had a deep desire to live their Truth and shine it outward. By their examples, they show us that it is possible for us to do the same.

Gandhi said, "You can do what I have done." Many other great masters and saints, such as the Buddha and Saint Francis of Assisi, have inspired us with that same message of hope.

I remember hearing this decades ago and thinking, *Really? I can do that?* For me, not only did I feel truly hopeful and inspired, I thought, *I have to do this, I want to do this.*

Every day when I sit down to read, I feel as if I am with an old friend walking this beautiful path of life. I am inspired to keep striving for peace within and becoming a beacon of light and love in the world.

Once I read a book, I move on to the next, but I can tell you there are some on the list in Appendix B that I have read dozens of times, with each sitting discovering something new or gaining a deeper insight. Recently, I reread *The Way of a Pilgrim,* a beautiful book about a Russian Orthodox pilgrim who sets out on a quest to learn how to "pray without ceasing." This partial sentence made me stop and take notice: "He eagerly begged me actually to show him the way the mind finds the heart, and how to find the joy of praying inwardly with the heart." This is what we are doing in the morning when we meditate and use our Sacred Mantra throughout the day. Our mind is finding the heart!

No matter how many times I read a book, there is always something "new" that touches my heart. My wish is that you find the same is true for you. Keep reading and enjoy.

> *"I have done what you can do. These things you can verify for yourself. This is an experiential path; undertake this experiment and discover the results for yourself."*
>
> —Buddha

WHEN TO READ FOR INSPIRATION. Read whenever you have the opportunity to sit down and be fully present to the words on the page. I find an excellent time for inspirational reading is just before doing the Reflection exercise in the Letting Go part of The Practice (see Chapter 3), or following your meditation practice. This is a practice, and finding the time at some point throughout the day may be difficult, so I carry a book in my purse or in the car and have it handy whenever the opportunity to read presents itself.

Reading for Inspiration is perfect when you are sitting at the doctor's office waiting for your appointment. Your mind becomes absorbed in the mystic or teacher instead of being agitated or stressed if your appointment is delayed. This reading keeps you in the present moment and, honestly, from being bored, which can be fertile time for the mind to take off into the future or regress to the past.

As you take up this practice, you will begin to notice that you are discovering more and more opportunities to read, even if it is just for a few minutes.

WHERE TO READ FOR INSPIRATION. Read anywhere and everywhere. I happen to love to read outside or on the beach. Be creative and find places and times that work for you; then incorporate reading into your day just as if you were scheduling lunch with a friend or a meeting with a coworker. Keep a book in the car, on your nightstand, or next to your meditation spot, for example.

HOW LONG TO READ FOR INSPIRATION. The whole objective is to try to get some reading time in every day. Over the years, I have found that reading for fifteen minutes each day is wonderfully inspiring and just what I need to stay connected to my "spiritual companions" on this path. That being said, I am flexible and accommodating to my schedule; some days I may read longer, and then there are those days when I have only enough time to read a sentence or a paragraph before I do my Reflection.

Committing to make this precious reading part of my day is what matters most, so even one sentence can be just the inspiration I need and the break my mind is looking for.

THE VALUE OF READING FOR INSPIRATION. Reading for Inspiration is different from reading a self-help book or a novel. Although there is great and necessary value in reading and learning about self-improvement techniques or reading exciting mysteries, many of the books on the reading list in this book are about the personal stories of these great beings and their showing us the way rather than telling us the way.

When we read about their lives and their truly personal heartaches and joys, we connect with them on a deep level. Many times when I am reading one of these books, I say to myself, *How did he know I needed to hear that?* or *Oh my gosh, she is speaking directly to me.* I bet you have had a similar experience.

Enjoying the Benefits
of Reading for Inspiration

When we take some time each day to immerse ourselves in the inspirational words of mystics, saints, spiritual masters, teachers, and other spiritually minded people, we are actively cultivating a peaceful mind. Reading inspirational and spiritual texts helps us to do the following:

- Overcome challenges in our own lives through examples
- Relax our body while exercising our mind spiritually
- Open our mind to different points of view and new possibilities
- Nourish our mind with positive messages
- Warm our heart and offer us hope that we can "do what others have done"
- Know we are not alone in our trials and tribulations
- Reinforce our resolve to make positive change in our lives
- Strengthen our devotion and discipline
- Get us in touch with a real sense of love

Parting Thoughts

"The journey is all there is, really. The future never comes, because it's always the present moment," said Pema Chödrön on a retreat I attended with her in 2009. The truth and significance of her words truly becomes clear when we make a consistent effort to live in the present moment and, as a result, discover the joy that resides there—in the now. We will no longer need to live for the future or dwell in the past. Instead, we live our lives fully and completely in the moment.

With The Practice, we do this by using our Sacred Mantra to keep us grounded throughout the day, by consistently practicing Focused Attention with everyone and everything, and by Reading for Inspiration. Now we can take a look at how we can let the past rest, and experience each new day as a gift, in the next chapter: Letting Go.

Takeaway Seeds

SEED 1   The Sacred Mantra is a word, phrase, verse, or prayer with a long history of use that is hallowed or considered holy by the tradition or culture from which it originated.

SEED 2   In your search for a Sacred Mantra, choose one that feels comfortable, that resonates with you on a deep level, and that touches your heart.

SEED 3   When our attention is focused, we are present to only what we are doing—we are honoring the moment by giving it our all.

SEED 4   The great masters lived from the inside out, and by their examples, they show us that it is possible for us to do the same.

SEED 5   The great masters inspire us to uncover the Truth that we too are incredible human beings.

Chapter 3

LETTING GO

Reflecting on the Day and Making Peace with Ourselves

*"Do you want to enjoy a symphony?
Don't hold on to a few bars of the music.
Don't hold on to a couple of notes.
Let them pass, let them flow.
The whole enjoyment of a symphony lies in your
readiness to allow the notes to pass."*

—Anthony de Mello

I n the quotation that opens this chapter, spiritual guide Anthony de Mello is asking us quite simply whether we want to enjoy life. And if we do, we cannot hold on to even a few moments of it. Our "enjoyment of a symphony" lies in our ability to let every moment, every thought, and every experience pass. Releasing the past, or letting go, is essential for our peace of mind, but what does it mean exactly and how is it done?

If letting go were a simple process, we would never hold grudges or yearn for the "good old days." Like everything, letting go takes practice and a conscious effort. How many times do you recall saying, "Oh, just let it go" or "I wish I could let go of that"? We make these statements all the time. It certainly seems that it is something we want to do, but we know it is not all that easy. What makes it even more difficult is that our minds are often moving at such speeds that we do not even know what we are holding on to—let alone how to let go of it.

For me, letting go simply means becoming aware of and releasing the thoughts and memories that our minds are clinging to—repetitive thoughts that focus on *couldhave, shouldhave, rememberwhen,* and *whatif.* When we are able to let go of ruminating about the past or worrying about the future, we can see the gifts and opportunities in the present moment. We are better able to recognize our blessings, even in the midst of our challenges and stress.

At times it may seem impossible to release the past and let go of worries and stress. It is not enough to say, "Oh, I am going to let go of that now," thinking it is the first step toward letting worrisome or stressful thoughts go. Remember, it is the nature of the mind to want to be in control, sometimes even at the expense of our happiness. It will keep us in its repetitive thought loop for as long as it can, which is why the structure of The Practice is so helpful.

Of course, we cannot begin to release anything until we look at what it is that we need to release, acknowledge it, change our thinking, and take what we need to learn from it. For this purpose, in The Practice we set aside a regular time each day to actively engage in an evening Reflection, which helps us release the events of the day. This is precisely how we take notice, increase our awareness, and become truly grateful for every day that we are alive.

REFLECTION

Reflection is our final exercise of the day. This is when we scan our day and "officially" let go of everything that happened in the day—all the ups and downs—so that we can wake up the next morning in the new day without attachments or regrets over what happened the day before. Without yesterday's worries and stresses weighing us down, we can begin a new day with a peaceful mind and heart.

There is really nothing specific you need to do to prepare for Reflection other than relax and get into bed. It is so interesting here to actually think about winding down and officially ending our day. Have you ever thought about doing this? Of course, you can do a number of things to wind down once the day is over. I start the process of ending my day with Reading for Inspiration. This is a wonderful way to shift from my busy outward thinking to spiritually nourishing inward thinking. This last practice of the day is meant to leave our day "in the day" and sleep peacefully knowing our day's work is done.

If we want to end our day quiet, centered, and peaceful, we must find a way to disconnect from the outer world. So this is not a good time to watch the news or read the newspaper. There is plenty of time to do that during the day. Remember, our point here is to close out the day. My usual nightly routine is this: I get into bed, do some inspirational reading, repeat my Sacred Mantra to stay focused, and then scan my day and reflect. Then as I drift off to sleep, I repeat my Sacred Mantra.

When I first began my nightly Reflection, I found it incredible just how unaware I had been during my days—how "asleep" I really was. I had been going through life from moment to moment without really noticing what I was doing or stopping to think before I acted. I began to see how easily I fell into a routine of living my life based on my conditioned habits and behaviors rather than living in a state of awareness, present to every moment in which I had the ability to make decisions and actually choose moment by moment.

When you start incorporating The Practice into your life, you will realize that in order to live a life fully alive and fully present to everyone and everything, you must become aware. Little by little, nightly Reflection helps you develop that awareness. This allows you to make the moment-by-moment choices that will lead you closer to the magnificent and loving life you are meant to live.

HOW LONG TO PRACTICE REFLECTION. Reflect for five to ten minutes. This part of The Practice is intentionally short because it is easy to get trapped into trying to figure out some things at the end of the day. The mind loves nothing better than to ruminate over what went wrong and how we could have done things better or smarter. But there is nothing to figure out. The day is over, so the idea is to notice, become aware, and move through it and not get stuck on any one part. We cannot change anything that has happened; we can only become aware of the happenings of our day and take notice of what we may learn by reflecting and then making a note of what we might want to do differently or similarly if given an opportunity another day.

WHEN TO PRACTICE REFLECTION. Do your Reflection at the end of the day, *after* you have done everything you need to do to prepare yourself to turn in for the night. The idea is to go straight to sleep when you are done. You are truly making an effort to close out the day and go to sleep knowing you have ended the day the best you can.

WHERE TO PRACTICE REFLECTION. I recommend practicing Reflection sitting up in your bed. That is where I do mine. If you have a special room or place set aside for your morning meditation, you can do your Reflection there, if you choose. It is usually best to keep the lights on so that the urge to fall asleep does not come over you before you are done reviewing your day. Wherever you decide to practice your Reflection, the key is to be ready to go straight to bed when you are finished.

HOW TO PRACTICE REFLECTION. Take a few deep breaths and relax. Then begin to visualize the events of the day in order as if you are watching a movie. As you scan the "frames," let the day easily pass through your mind without judgment.

Your mind may want to get stuck on certain events: *Why did I do that? Why did I say that? I should have done or said this instead.* That is its nature, so simply take notice of the event and gently repeat your Sacred Mantra as needed to get back on track and guide it along. There is nothing you can do to change what occurred during the past twenty-four hours; this is a great revelation for us. I know there are times I am reflecting on my day when my mind tries to convince me that I can actually change the events and outcomes of the day. We all know that this cannot be; what is done is done. But we can become aware and then make an intention to handle things differently the next day.

Remember, this is not a judging exercise; we are simply noticing. The moment we start to judge, we lose our ability to eventually let go. Let me state this another way: When we start to judge ourselves or others, we immediately get stuck, making it impossible to "let go" of the day. So make an effort to really be present to these particular memories running through the mind, and try not to get stuck on any of them. Look at everything. Then as they pass, make an intention to release them.

It really is not necessary to make your Reflection so detailed that you do a moment-by-moment replay. For me, it is nearly impossible to remember every little detail of my day, no matter how present I might have been. Actually, I have found that trying to remember the specific details has many times interfered with my ability to move forward and let go of the day. For example, when I do my Reflection, I do not try to re-create the whole day. I reflect on "events" such as my walk with my dog, my first interaction with my husband in the morning, my afternoon meeting, my experience at the dentist, or my phone call with my sister. I try to break down the day into segments and look at the highlights.

Naturally, if it has been a particularly disturbing day, those memories come up quite easily. The same is true when the day has been wonderful; that, too, is easy to reflect on. In either case—difficult day or wonderful day—the whole purpose of this precious time is to let the day go so you are ready to start the following day fresh. This is truly a beautiful gift.

The Art of Noticing Without Judgment

We cannot change what happened during the day, but our minds often try to rewrite the ending by thinking about how it should have or could have gone differently. We sometimes go to sleep just racked with guilt, pain, stress, anger, or suffering: Why did I do this? Why did this happen to me? I should have done this. I could have done that. Why did they treat me this way? I feel so guilty for saying those negative things. I'm so angry with her/him! This is not right, what happened to me!

But really, what does this do for us? It actually puts us into an agitated, unsettled place just before sleep. Can you see the absurdity in stressing ourselves out before bed? Here we are, especially after a hard day, thinking, *Oh good, the day is over and I can finally end it by going to sleep,* but then the mind ruminates over what happened, and there is no way we are getting to sleep; it is impossible. We can only find peace when we are able to let the day go. I know this sounds easier said than done, but little by little, with practice, we become able to leave the day in the day, knowing we did the best we could.

The beauty of life is that it repeats itself. Even though we cannot change what happened on any particular day, chances are we will probably have another opportunity to try again in a similar situation. So we leave whatever it was in that day, but with the awareness and knowledge that we will most likely have another opportunity. Then when that opportunity presents itself, we will make the connection: Oh, this is where I have the opportunity to try this out a little bit differently and see what happens. For example, if I am looking at my day and I see a part where I was impatient with my daughter, I can reflect on the reasons for my impatience: Oh, yes, I was trying to make dinner and something was about to burn, but then the phone rang at the same time my daughter asked me a question, and I snapped at her and said, "Go ask your father!"

When I reflect on this, I am not blaming or chastising myself for my impatience or for being angry with my daughter for interrupting me. I am just acknowledging that I was impatient; in that simple acknowledgment, the new action comes. I now see that next time I could just let my daughter know I would need a few moments before I could respond to her, unless it was an emergency. Phone calls can always go to voice mail if I have to attend to something on the stovetop. In this way, I can see how by Living Present, in the moment, a different response could be beneficial to both my loved ones and myself.

Many of us can relate to being pulled in many directions during the moments of our day. For example, during Reflection, you may notice that you did not handle something as well as you would have liked. Again, this is not about making excuses; it is, however, about acknowledging those factors that may have contributed to your inability to handle matters the way you would have liked—factors such as not getting enough sleep, skipping breakfast, or putting too much pressure and stress on yourself.

Noticing interactions like this is how you begin to tap into your inner wisdom and knowledge. This gives you the perfect opportunity to make an intention to handle something differently next time or to make a change if necessary. You become aware or, as the Buddha said, awake.

QUESTIONS FOR REFLECTION. When it comes to Reflection, some people have no difficulty visualizing the events of the day and spending a thoughtful moment or two on the highs and the lows. Others prefer prompts to jog their memories and help them focus their thoughts. I have had many people during my workshops ask me for sample questions, so if the latter is your preference, the following are some questions you can use when performing your nightly review.

When responding to the questions, just observe your answers without judgment. These questions are intended as examples to help you acknowledge and release your day:

- ⤜ Did I give my full attention to the people in my life?
- ⤜ Was I present for them? Was I patient with them?
- ⤜ How was my interaction with my family and friends?
- ⤜ How was my interaction with my coworkers and acquaintances?
- ⤜ Did I make eye contact with people?
- ⤜ Did I listen to what others had to say?
- ⤜ Did I use The Practice in my day? How did it help?
- ⤜ Did I turn to my Sacred Mantra for support?
- ⤜ What went well today?
- ⤜ What didn't go well today?
- ⤜ What are my blessings?

COMPLETING YOUR REFLECTION. When you have completed your review of the events of your day, a nice way to seal the process is by repeating an affirmation. You can write one for yourself, or, if it resonates with you, you may want to use the affirmation that follows, which was written and used by my dear friend Mary for this part of The Practice. If you choose an affirmation of your own, which you are likely to want to do as your practice progresses, just be sure that it centers on being present and releasing the day so that your mind knows it is time to let go.

"This day is now over. I choose to live in the present moment. I am thankful for having been given this day and the blessings that it has held. I take comfort in now releasing any challenges or successes I experienced today, and I head into a restful sleep with the peace and knowledge that tomorrow is a new day. I am always working toward the person I wish to be."

We often take for granted that tomorrow will come, and, of course, there is a good chance it will. Although this may be true, I always keep in mind that there is never a foolproof guarantee we will wake up in the morning. This may sound difficult for some to hear spoken, but for me, it feels quite the opposite. Keeping this in mind reminds me of how precious each day is and helps me focus more on the positives than on the negatives.

Some years ago, I spent time in Mexico on a service project to build an orphanage and school for a small village. I had the great privilege to hear a Native American speak who, at the time, was seventy-eight years old and in extremely good health. Both his mother and his grandmother were still alive! During the Q&A time, a teenager asked him how he accounted for his longevity, to which he replied, "I do not drink soda, and I wake up every morning in the new day. I let the day go to sleep with me at night, never knowing if I am going to wake up the next morning. So if I do wake up, I am so happy that I have a great day in front of me . . . even if it's not such a 'great' day."

The words of this wise man continue to touch my heart because I understand on a deep level just how true they are. In 2007, my first husband (my daughter's father) went to sleep one night and did not wake up. We can never really be certain that we will wake up tomorrow. This is not meant to be scary. It is meant to be a mindful and thoughtful reminder: live each day to the fullest and make an effort to be our greatest self so that we will always remember that every day we are given is a precious gift. Our Reflection time before bed is truly meant to be a time to express our sincere thankfulness for that gift.

But what if you had a particularly bad day? What if someone did something to you that you think is unforgivable? A situation like this is a good time to call upon your Sacred

Mantra for additional support. You may even want to take a few minutes to write out your Sacred Mantra with the intention of healing the situation or your feelings surrounding the person or area of concern. I find this practice extraordinarily helpful when I have had a particularly trying day. Writing your Sacred Mantra is discussed in more detail in Chapter 4.

The same way you will notice that there were things about your day that you were not so happy about, you will also notice the highlights. You might find yourself saying, *Oh, wow, I handled that really well! This was a fabulous day; I really wish it would not end.* That is great, of course, but let that go, too. Just notice it, smile, and embrace the happiness for the moment, and then let it pass along with the rest of the day. This is not about judging things good or bad. It is simply a way to acknowledge events, gain wisdom from the lessons they offered, and then let them go. Success is going to bed at night knowing you did the best job you could, feeling truly at peace with yourself.

> *"This is a unique moment. Maybe I'm glad about that because it's painful, but I don't want to waste it, because it's never going to happen again this way."*
>
> —Pema Chödrön

GRATITUDE FOR
THE BLESSINGS

When I first read *On Death and Dying* by Elisabeth Kübler-Ross in the late eighties, I was deeply touched by the five stages of grief—denial, anger, bargaining, depression, and acceptance. I was going through a traumatic separation from my first husband, and I immediately felt that Kübler-Ross was speaking to me in my current situation and that the concepts she wrote about could be brilliantly applied to any loss we experience in life, not just death. As I read through each stage, I nodded in agreement. I had felt the denial, the anger, the bargaining, and now the depression, all of which an imminent divorce brings up. Still, I wondered exactly how I would ever get to the stage of acceptance.

It took some time, but I was eventually able to arrive at a place of acceptance, of letting go. As I emerged from the pain of my divorce, I understood what Kübler-Ross meant when she wrote, "There are no mistakes, no coincidences, all events are blessings to us to learn from." The beauty of reaching this stage was that I could see the blessings amid the chaos and difficulty of my divorce, and I found great joy in my life again. I was grateful for the lessons I had learned. Keep in mind that I was not grateful for the tragedy, but rather for the blessings it revealed.

Loss of any kind can feel tragic while we are going through it, but we often look at death as the ultimate tragedy. We have such a fear of it and of the unknown in general. And when we are talking about spirituality, death is naturally somewhere in the equation. After all, death is the ultimate "letting go."

As a child, I was the designated "funeral-goer" with my father, and I always attended the funerals with great curiosity and reverence. It was hard for me to grasp the thought that I would never see the person again. My presence at these funerals set me on a quest to understand death and learn the answer to the question: "Exactly where do we go when we die?" After my decades of practice, I have come to love and ascribe to the following teaching from the Bhagavad Gita (chapter 2, verse 12): "Never was there a time when I did not exist, nor you, nor all these kings; nor in the future shall any of us cease to be."

Never has this verse been so important to me than it is right now. During the writing of this book, my dad passed away at age seventy-nine. He had always been active and healthy, so when my brother called to tell me that Dad did not look well and was rapidly losing weight, I dropped everything to go visit him in southern Indiana. He did look awful—he was much thinner, his speech was slurred, and he was in pain. He had been to many doctors, but they could not give him a diagnosis.

This situation was frustrating, to say the least, largely because it was most certainly out of my control. I called upon my Sacred Mantra quite often during that time and focused on being present for my dad. My daughter and I spent a few wonderful days with him, and then we flew home.

Two weeks later, I got the call that he had been rushed to the hospital in Cincinnati, Ohio. Once again, I dropped everything and went to his side. He was very sick. After my dad spent a week in the hospital, the doctors determined that he was in the advanced stages of ALS (amyotrophic lateral sclerosis). I knew his time was coming to an end, so I spent the bulk of his remaining twenty days with him until he passed away peacefully.

When my dad died, I was the only one in the hospital room. It was a stormy day, the windows were shaking, the nurses were scared, and the heavy rain, lightning, and thunder were causing quite a ruckus in the hospital. I told them I lived in Florida and these afternoon thunderstorms were common. Deep within me, I knew my dad was dying—the storm seemed somewhat symbolic to me—and I knew I was ready for what was to come. But was I *really* ready to let my dad go? Did I want to acknowledge the truth that he was dying?

Can we ever truly be completely ready for the death of a loved one? I had been working toward this for decades, the perfectionist in me. I was, after all, the "funeral-goer" in the family, and I had been practicing and studying spiritual teachings for so many years. My mind knows that we are not the body, and I knew that my dad's spirit, his soul, would always live on and that he would always be with me. Still, I was completely shocked in that moment when he stopped breathing. My heart ached. *Is he really gone? But wait, it can't be; it is too soon. He looks so beautiful, so peaceful.*

My dad died on July 18, 2012. Of course, time has healed the physical loss, and I know I feel his presence—"nor in the future shall any of us cease to be." When our mind, body, and heart are united, we know deeply that we are not the body. Our essence can never die.

I love this beautiful quote a friend sent me in a sympathy card; it touched my heart and made me break out in a big smile. *The perfect analogy,* I thought to myself. "Even though we cannot see the bird singing in the forest, we can still hear his song." Death gives us the perfect opportunity to have faith in the unseen.

Enjoying the Benefits of Reflection

"Finish each day and be done with it. You have done what you could; some blunders and absurdities have crept in; forget them as soon as you can. Tomorrow is a new day; you shall begin it serenely and with too high a spirit to be encumbered with your old nonsense," said Ralph Waldo Emerson. When we take the time each evening to reflect on our day and then let it drift away as we fall asleep, we will be opening ourselves up to receive the benefits of this nightly practice. These benefits include helping us to do the following:

- ⤳ Release any guilt we may have felt as a result of our actions or inactions that day
- ⤳ Reveal the blessings and gifts in our daily lives so that we can feel gratitude
- ⤳ Increase our self-awareness so that we start to know ourselves better
- ⤳ Change unhealthy behaviors in the day to follow
- ⤳ Begin a new day being present and unattached to yesterday

Parting Thoughts

When we regularly observe and reflect, we become a little wiser, a little more awake and aware every day. Reflection is a beautiful way to seal our practice—to close up the day. Remember, we can never *really* be sure that we will have a new day ahead. That is a sobering thought: to live every day as if it might be our last. This is why it is so important for us to be present to each moment of our lives and to express our gratitude for each new day.

So really the whole point is this: Close your day, close your practice, and close your life for that day. If it happens to be your destiny to have another day, you can start the new day fresh without attachments or regrets. A Native American friend says this profoundly simple prayer to end her day: *My day is done. I turn myself over to you, Great Spirit, and goodnight.*

Takeaway Seeds

SEED 1   To "let go" simply means to release the thoughts and memories that our minds are clinging to.

SEED 2   The purpose of Reflection is to make peace with yourself at the end of the day, so that you can be present, aware, and grateful for the day ahead.

SEED 3   Even though we cannot change what happened, we will probably have another chance to try again in a similar situation.

SEED 4   Reflection is a way to acknowledge events, gain wisdom, and then let them go.

SEED 5   Finding gratitude is not about being grateful for the tragedy; it is about being grateful for the blessings that helped us grow as a result of that tragedy.

CHAPTER 4

DEEPENING THE PRACTICE

Tending to Our Spiritual Care and Support

"When your consciousness is directed outward, mind and world arise. When it is directed inward, it realizes its own Source and returns home into the Unmanifested."

—Eckhart Tolle

Incorporating The Practice or even just parts of it into our daily lives sheds a light on our inner selves, giving us a deeper look inside. With that added awareness, we can start to make the positive changes we have always wanted to make and lead the magnificent life we have always wanted to live. This chapter is dedicated to all the ways that we can deepen our experience of The Practice.

Each of the activities described in this chapter is a powerful adjunct to the spiritual framework provided by The Practice. Most of these activities complement the Living Present part of our day, since the idea is to actively and mindfully engage the task. This is great practice for Focused Attention.

When we take the time to give ourselves this additional spiritual care and support, the many benefits of The Practice are enhanced and strengthened. You will notice a difference in your meditation, since many of these activities improve your ability to concentrate. It is my hope that the activities I do in my life and share with you in this chapter will help you to further deepen your connection to yourself and bring you greater meaning and joy.

The brilliant German mystic Meister Eckhart said, "Go into your own ground and learn to know yourself there." This is your life; your spiritual journey is unique to you, so have fun trying out these suggestions and discover for yourself what enhances and deepens your spiritual practice and your life.

GETTING TO KNOW YOUR MIND

If you were not aware before, you certainly know now that our minds are constantly going, and most of the time we are not paying attention to the chatter. If you need a reminder of what is going on "up there," take another look at the illustration of the mind on page 59. As shown in the illustration, our minds often focus on worst-case scenarios, on our faults and weaknesses and those of others, on the mistakes we have made, and on our concerns about the future. That is the mind's nature, of course, but it is also the cause of a lot of our suffering and stress.

To reduce the suffering that mind-chatter causes us and to take back control of our thoughts, we simply need to start by paying close attention to the thoughts in the mind and getting to know the mind better. This is the only way we can really discover what is going on in there.

For this exercise, set aside a few moments throughout the day to listen to whatever is on your mind closely and without judgment. Just observe. The more you listen, the more you realize that much of what your mind is focusing on is in the past, is out of your control, or has not even happened yet. The more you listen, the more you realize that a lot of what your mind is telling you much of the time is nonsense. Often now, as a result of "getting to know my mind very well," instead of becoming caught up in these thoughts, I laugh at the absurdity. *This just is not true,* I tell my mind. *Please leave.*

A variation of this activity is to jot down your thoughts in a notebook. I often find that seeing my thoughts on paper has an even greater impact on me. Whether we write down our thoughts or not, we are shining a light on what is going on inside our mind. With this greater awareness, we can start redirecting our thoughts to the present moment in which we have a choice. Most of the time when I bring my mind out of the thoughts of the past or future, I feel a great sense of knowing that "all is well" in this moment.

PUTTING WORRIES
INTO PERSPECTIVE

We all worry. The greatest problem with worry is that much of the time we end up worrying about things that never happen or just really are not as bad as we think they will be. When we look back, we often see that we have made mountains out of molehills.

For this exercise, you will need a "worry notebook." Make a list of things you are worried might happen in the upcoming week. Jot down the best- and worst-case scenarios in your notebook. Then, a week later, go back to your list and review it. Were any of your worries proven? Or were most unfounded? Chances are you will discover that seldom, if ever, do the worst-case scenarios you imagined come true.

A variation of this activity is to list all your expectations—both bad and good—for the week ahead. When you revisit the list a week later, make a note of how many of those events turned out the way you expected.

Doing this exercise from time to time helps us to see just how much time and energy we waste worrying about things that never materialize or do not turn out the way we expect. We slowly start to realize that all this worrying saps our energy and strength, leaving us tired, stressed, and unhappy. When we start to become aware, we are able to put our worries into perspective, reclaim our time and energy, and begin living in the present—happy and well.

SACRED MANTRA WRITING

The Sacred Mantra is a powerful tool, as discussed in Chapter 2, that helps us redirect our thoughts, clear our minds, and gain our focus. It can be called upon as often as it is needed throughout the day and is a source of strength and spiritual support.

Because the Sacred Mantra is powerful, the single-pointed exercise of writing it regularly improves our concentration and helps to strengthen our faith and trust in life. It is a deep, concentrated exercise with benefits that spill over into all other areas of The Practice.

I have filled many notebooks over the years with my Sacred Mantra: *My God and My All.* It is difficult to explain in words the benefits of performing Sacred Mantra writing, so I urge you to try it and discover it for yourself. See a sample page from one of my notebooks on the following page to give you a better idea of what this exercise looks like.

To do this activity, choose one concern or worry you have and write it at the top of a piece of paper or on a clean page in your notebook. Begin writing your Sacred Mantra. Go ahead and fill the page (or more, if you would like)! As you write your Sacred Mantra, focus your attention on the writing of your mantra, and when your mind starts to wander to something else, gently bring it back to your mantra and your intention of sending loving energy to the situation or person. I have felt a profound sense of peace and love come over me at the end of my writing.

If this activity resonates with you, you can perform it any time you or someone you love needs support for a specific challenge or just to send someone loving positive thoughts. You can use it to gain clarity, to find forgiveness, or to recognize the lesson or silver lining in a trying situation or tragedy. In many cases, this will most likely take some time, so be patient. Remember knowing something in our heads is the beginning; it may need time to get to our hearts.

Writing the Sacred Mantra helps facilitate that transformation. I spent nearly six years writing a page of my Sacred Mantra once a day for a particular situation in which I set the intention to forgive someone who had seriously hurt me. This may seem like a very long time, but one day, the situation came into my mind, and I was no longer emotionally charged. The thoughts came in and went out without a single irritation, sadness, or hurt feeling. I had found the forgiveness.

Forgiveness is a major issue in our lives; it has the power to keep us from being truly happy and whole. I could write an entire book on forgiveness. For now, let me share with you what I learned in 2007 when I was on a retreat with the Dalai Lama for a week in Indiana; it completely changed my way of thinking about forgiveness. During the question-and-answer time, a woman asked him, "Your Holiness, how do we forget what has happened to us so that we can forgive, and how do *you* forget what happened to you as a result of Tibet?"

With that cute smile and childlike expression, the Dalai Lama thought for a moment and then replied, "I don't forget, but I have forgiven."

I get goose bumps when I recall that moment, because for a long time I thought I had to forget what happened in order to forgive. And no matter how much I practiced my spiritual disciplines, I was having a hard time forgetting things that had been done to me in my life that were unkind. I know most of us have had things happen to us that were unkind and hurtful. I believed this inability to forget what had happened was a barrier to my ability to forgive. But his Holiness said that we don't want to *forget* the lessons we have learned, because forgetting could possibly put us in harm's way.

As I recall, he explained that a child learns not to go into a cage with a tiger because he could get killed; this is a lesson the child does not want to forget. For him, he said (and I am paraphrasing) that although he keeps his distance from the Chinese, he still wants peace; he practices loving-kindness and compassion for them.

Learning this teaching from the Dalai Lama changed my life. I did not need to erase the memories. My Sacred Mantra writing allowed me to embrace the feelings, and then I released the negative emotions attached to the events, eventually bringing forgiveness.

Forgiveness is defined as the ability to forgive. *To forgive* means to give up resentment or the desire to retaliate. Notice that there is nothing in this definition about forgetting. It is simply about no longer feeling as if we have to get even. It certainly does not mean we must welcome back hurtful people or harmful situations into our lives. Keeping the lessons in mind makes us more aware and helps us to keep away from potentially harmful encounters, hurtful people, and negative experiences—or at least it helps us make wise choices and respond differently in the future.

I sometimes write my Sacred Mantra for myself for help overcoming a particular challenge, issue, or obstacle. For instance, when my daughter, Michelle, was in college, I filled over 100 books in the four years she was away. In the beginning, I wrote mostly for the loss I felt at her absence as well as for her safety. By the beginning of her third year, I noticed a shift had occurred within me, and my fear and worry had disappeared. At that point, writing my mantra for her became about sending love, light, and goodness her way.

Often I write my Sacred Mantra for someone who is having a hard time, is sick, or has passed away, or for the tragedies that happen in the world. When the tsunami hit Indonesia in 2004, I felt it in my heart to start writing for everyone involved, sending them all the love in my heart. Before I knew it, I had written my Sacred Mantra for two hours.

When something horrific is happening or has happened, how often do we say to ourselves, *I wish there was something I could do*? Well, this is my way of feeling as if I am offering the situation as much love, Focused Attention, and compassion as possible. When I put that intention out there into the world, I *know* that this small action matters. As Gandhi said, "What we do may seem too small to matter, but it matters greatly that we do it." Not only do I believe deeply that I am helping others, the incredible transformation from within that results from writing my Sacred Mantra has been truly amazing and powerful in my life.

Here is a story that I like to share regarding Sacred Mantra writing that concerned a friend who was in flight during the tragic terrorist attacks of September 11, 2001. The passengers were informed that they could not land in New York but were not told why. Then the plane was diverted to Canada, where they were filled in on all the tragic events that had occurred.

My friend and the other passengers ended up being on that plane for almost a full day. Later, when we spoke, he told me that writing his Sacred Mantra for all those hours "saved my life."

Understandably, everyone on the plane was scared, irritated, and tired. Many were agitated and angry. My friend was able to maintain a calmness and sense of well-being with the help of his Sacred Mantra, and he told me his calmness spilled over to the people around him. He was teaching Sacred Mantra writing to his new friends on the plane.

Writing the Sacred Mantra truly is a remarkable practice; it deepens your intimacy with the verse or phrase. Please do not take my word for it. Try it today and every day. You may even get hooked, as I am.

SACRED MANTRA ART

A deeply satisfying way to use the Sacred Mantra is through the creation of artwork. This is much like Sacred Mantra writing and carries the same benefits. However, in this activity, instead of filling pages, the mantra is written within the spaces of a line drawing in various colors. It is like coloring with words. To give you a better idea of what this activity is all about, take a look at a sample Sacred Mantra artwork of mine. (To experience these in full color, which is quite a sight to behold, please visit my website at www.barbschmidt.com.)

I personally love this activity and have created hundreds of unique mandalas and designs. I make Sacred Mantra artwork for friends who are ill or have lost loved ones, and I have made them for people who need encouragement, or I simply give them as a gift for special occasions. When Michelle went off to college, I made one for her to hang on her wall. Her friends liked it so much I made some for them as well.

For this activity, you will need a clean line drawing on white paper and thin-tipped colored markers or sharp colored pencils. Write your mantra in the spaces, filling as much of the white space as possible with the words. Repeat the mantra to yourself as you write it. Plan your colors, switching off as necessary to create the design you want. You are an artist and maybe did not even realize it. This is such an incredibly beautiful way to express love to others, from the inside out.

You can keep the finished product or give it to a loved one or friend as a birthday, graduation, or sympathy card. Often, I make homemade cards with my mantra art and include a message or inspirational quotation inside. When a dear friend of mine had cancer surgery, I sent her a mantra card with an inspiring message and then wrote my personal words that included, "I have written my Sacred Mantra, *My God and My All* for you, blessing you and sending you my love."

Sacred Mantra art is a powerful activity that not only deepens your intimacy and connection with your mantra, it connects you deeply to those you are creating it for. Again, I say experience this for yourself and undertake this amazing journey.

LISTENING PRACTICE

What does it feel like when someone you are with gives you his or her Focused Attention—you know, when you are speaking to someone, and he or she is really listening to what you are saying? Wonderful, right? That is something we all want. And we want to be there for others that way as well. Often, though, it seems as if we are somewhere else, and I used the example earlier of when you forget someone's name almost the second you hear it.

It is not about forgetfulness. It is all about not having been fully present in the moment. Like most things, giving someone our undivided attention is not at all easy and takes practice.

To try this listening activity, you will need one or more partners. Each of you will take turns sharing whatever it is that you want to share with the other person or people. It can be anything: something that happened that day, something about your life, or whatever comes to mind. Each person speaks for one minute. (Use a gentle timer.)

During the minute, the listeners simply listen without asking questions. When the timer goes off, the next person goes. After each person has had an opportunity to take a turn, ask yourself the following questions: *How did it feel to be giving someone my full attention? Did my mind wander? Did I feel as if I was listening closely? When I was the speaker, did I feel as if I was speaking with full attention? How did it feel to get full attention?*

The great benefit of this activity is gaining firsthand awareness of what it feels like to be fully present for another person. Knowing how it feels to give someone your undivided attention makes it easier to shift your focus back to the present when your mind starts wandering or commenting. I love to do this activity with my friends and in our workshops. We laugh, we share, and we witness the incredible value and blessings of living in the present with the people in our lives.

STUDYING WITH
THE MASTERS

Reading for inspiration ideally should be a peaceful, undemanding time. But if you have a little extra time, and you are looking for extra depth in your reading, consider this activity: Begin by identifying a book that you find particularly inspirational. When you come across a paragraph that speaks to you, write it down in a notebook. Then, below that paragraph, jot down your own thoughts on its meaning. What do you think that great sage, mystic, or master is saying? Write whatever comes to mind. As you continue reading this book, identify and copy other inspirational paragraphs as well and continue to add your own commentary.

After a time of doing this, you will find that it is almost as if you are in class with that particular teacher. Imagine studying the yoga sutras with Patanjali himself! It is wonderfully uplifting to feel this close to the masters. Merton scholar James Finley suggests choosing one book and doing this activity for an entire year. I chose Saint Teresa of Avila's incredible book *The Interior Castle,* and I felt a complete shift; I now deeply understood what interior work, or going within, means. This is described in *The Interior Castle* as "going through the mansions." I was a student of Saint Teresa of Avila for a year of my life—what a blessing for me.

Simply stated, this transformative activity brings the book and author to life and deepens our understanding of his or her message, helping us truly live it in our daily lives.

CULTIVATING YOUR GARDEN

Earlier in the book, I mentioned that the idea of a meditation practice is to cultivate our minds the way we would cultivate a flower garden—by planting the plants we want, tending to them regularly, and keeping the ground fertile. This activity carries this analogy a little further. Create a bountiful garden by cultivating the "flowers" of presence for others: gratitude, kindness, and patience. Here are some ideas for watering your garden.

PRESENCE FOR OTHERS. The next time the phone rings, give the caller your complete attention. This means not washing dishes, cleaning up, checking e-mails, surfing the Internet, and so on—whatever you might do that will distract you from the person on the other end of the line. I often fight the instinct to use the time more "wisely." If something needs to be attended to, I will let the person know I cannot talk right now. But if I choose to be on the phone, I sit down and make it my intention to give that person my complete attention. Sometimes I find that closing my eyes helps. This is truly Living Present. Try it. You may find it quite difficult but very rewarding.

GRATITUDE. During the day, I often take a minute to breathe deeply and say thank you—*thank you for my life.* I may think of specific things I am thankful for or just take the minute to remember what a gift this day is and how fortunate I am to be alive. While it only takes a minute to do this, the gratitude I feel is long lasting. From time to time throughout the day, think about what you have to be grateful for. This powerful act has the amazing ability to transform your thoughts in just a matter of moments.

KINDNESS. "Be kind, be kind, be kind." This is the motto of my life. I practice loving-kindness as often as possible. As the Dalai Lama has said, "The more you nurture a feeling of loving-kindness, the happier and calmer you will be." Think about ways to show a kindness, such as letting someone move ahead of you while waiting in a grocery line, smiling at a stranger, or offering help to someone you see is struggling. When I am walking in a big city, such as Chicago, where my daughter lives, I often say my mantra as I am walking down the street and look into the eyes of everyone walking past me. I get this warmhearted feeling that we are all on this planet together.

PATIENCE. In all the little things in life, I try to have an attitude of patience. When it comes to patience, driving is a great lesson for me. Sometimes when I am in traffic, I begin to get annoyed by the other drivers and find myself thinking, *Why is this person driving so slow? How inconsiderate of them! I have somewhere to be.* As soon as I recognize my agitation, I immediately begin repeating my Sacred Mantra and often move into the right lane where the drivers are slower. It stops the speed of the negative thoughts, and I start to feel calmer and less stressed.

Having patience in these ordinary moments of my day helps me cultivate patience in similar situations. Instead of letting my mind be agitated, I practice patience with the repetition of my Sacred Mantra. This line from a Saint Teresa of Avila prayer, "Patience attains all things," sums it up beautifully. I know that when I am patient I am happy.

Quotations
Notebook

I find it nourishing to start my day with words of inspiration. One of the most wonderful comments we hear regularly from our Peaceful Mind Peaceful Life Facebook and e-mail friends is how deeply inspired they are by our quotations and pictures. One young girl said recently, "I look forward to starting my day with your inspirational words."

If this appeals to you, you may want to start a notebook to collect some of your favorites. When a quote you come across touches you deeply, jot it down in your notebook. (Remember to include the author so you know the origins of the quote.) You may also like to write a sentence about what that particular thought means to you.

Visit our Facebook page (https://www.facebook.com/peacefulmindpeacefullife), where we post inspirational quotes throughout the day. You will also find a treasure of inspiration in the books on the inspirational reading list. Just think, if you do this regularly, your notebook will soon be filled with the words of the great masters, saints, teachers, and mystics of the world. When the words from a great inspirational being touch us deeply, it is because they spark something deep within our consciousness. We can return to that place whenever we reread and think about the message.

Often a quotation can become a model for how we wish to live our life. For example, Gandhi's statement "Be the change you wish to see in the world" is the motto of Peaceful Mind Peaceful Life. The moment I heard it, my body shivered. It touched me so deeply that I knew I wanted to live that way. I wanted to be an example of the world I wished to someday see.

Now whenever I am faced with a choice, this quote comes up. I ask myself which decision will help me move toward my wish for the world and which will take me farther away from it. In every instance, I choose the one that will take me closer to a world of unity, loving-kindness, and compassion for all beings. A quote journal may be the spark to help you identify a high ideal for your life. At the very least, it is a fabulous way to gather inspiration.

LIKE-MINDED GROUPS

When we are trying to live a structured spiritual life, it helps to be around others who are focused on nurturing their own spirituality. I am blessed to have such a group. For the past thirteen years, I have been teaching a meditation class in Boca Raton, Florida. Of all the things I do in my life, this is one of my top five. I only miss it for hurricanes and other emergencies! For the first hour and a half, we talk and share our lives through the lens of great inspirational books, authors, saints, masters, and mystics. Then in the final half hour we meditate together. This is powerful, inspiring, and a special time for all of us.

Connecting weekly with like-minded people can be amazingly supportive. Let's face it: our lives are fast paced and technologically based and mostly drive us to look outward at the external world. During this weekly time together, we have the opportunity to go within and leave the outside world *outside* for that precious time. We gain strength, inspiration, and wisdom from the time we spend together by discussing and focusing on the world within. Then when it is time to leave, we feel grounded and ready to face the world with love, strength, and knowledge.

We relate to one another from the heart. What is amazing is that we are all so close, but we barely know anything about one another's external lives. There is something magical about lovingly connecting to another being just because!

You may wish to join a group of like-minded people to support you on your spiritual journey. See if you can find a meditation group or group of people you relate to who meet for the purpose of living a life from within. If you cannot find one, consider starting one of your own. You only need yourself and another person to start a group. In the early days, we had a small group of maybe three or four people. These days, we often have up to twenty-five. We have almost outgrown the room. The old adage "If you start it, they will come," is true. So have patience and perseverance as you reach out for support.

Another group of like-minded people can be found in your inspirational reading. Remember, the saints, masters, and mystics were just like us. Reading their life stories can be an incredible source of bonding. When we have a deep desire for living the magnificent life we are meant to live—happy, loving, and strong—we can find a way to be supported on our spiritual journey. Be creative, open, and receptive, and you will find it. We are never alone in this.

You may also wish to join the Peaceful Mind Peaceful Life community, where inspiration and support is available at your fingertips. You can follow the blog at http://peacefulmind-peacefullife.org/blog and sign up for daily inspirational quotes. If you are on Facebook, I invite you to join our Facebook community as well.

"Imagine that every person in the world is enlightened
but you. They are all your teachers, each doing
just the right things to help you learn perfect patience,
perfect wisdom, perfect compassion."

—Anthony de Mello

Spreading the Seeds
of Peace Throughout
Our Communities

We live in an outside world, not a cave. At some point, we will want to use what we have gained by going within to benefit our families and our communities. Little by little, by changing ourselves, we change the world. When we deepen our connection to our source through spiritual practices, we naturally become peacemakers and peace builders.

Whenever you are thinking, *This little thing that I am doing to improve myself is not going to make a darn bit of difference in the whole scheme of things,* think again. It is going to make a huge difference. The eighteenth-century philosopher Edmund Burke said, "Nobody made a greater mistake than he who did nothing because he could only do a little." I believe that we should never forget that every little bit counts. And as anthropologist Jane Goodall said at one of Peaceful Mind Peaceful Life's lectures several years ago, "We must remember, each and every one of us, that our voices and our actions make a difference every day." How much more convincing do we need? Great spiritual masters have been telling us this for centuries.

When we interact with the world from a grounded place— that sacred space inside us—we are living from the inside out. We can be strong, confident, and loving. We do not give our power over to anything, but instead we use our power to make change, to make a difference in the outside world. As Caroline Myss says, "There is no such thing as a simple act of compassion or an inconsequential act of service. Everything we do for another person has infinite consequences."

I founded Peaceful Mind Peaceful Life as a movement of beautiful human beings wishing to bring peace, love, and mindfulness to our world. We are embodying Gandhi's view: "Be the change you wish to see in the world." I urge you to find passion in your life that causes you to be of service to others. When we can be of service, we come out of ourselves and find that we are beings of great responsibility, and we learn by example that what "we do for another person has infinite consequences" for that person and ourselves. By changing our-selves "from the inside out," we become magnificent beings, strong, loving, and confident.

We are intentionally changing ourselves and thus bring-ing change to the world, in our daily, quiet, beautiful way—a movement that inspires us to be loving, happy, serving, laugh-ing; one of kindness and compassion, because if anything matters, then everything matters.

Parting Thoughts

The spiritual journey is multifaceted. There are many paths to the same destination and much support along the road if we seek it out. The activities and suggestions in this chapter are intended to help you deepen your connection to your inner source. Through The Practice and sharing your inner gift of peace with the people in your life, you will discover the happiness and fulfillment you seek.

Takeaway Seeds

SEED 1　When we put our worries into perspective, we can start to reclaim our time and energy and begin living in the present.

SEED 2　The Sacred Mantra is powerful, and writing it regularly strengthens our faith and trust in life.

SEED 3　When the words of a great inspirational being touch us deeply, it is because they spark something deep within our consciousness.

SEED 4　Connecting weekly with like-minded people can be amazingly supportive.

SEED 5　When we deepen our connection to our source through spiritual practices, we naturally become peacemakers and peace builders.

Conclusion

> "*Don't cry because it's over, smile because it happened.*"
>
> —Dr. Seuss

L ife is a journey that we take step by step—sometimes carefully, sometimes headlong. We are often so busy "doing" that we forget that our first nature is to *be*. The Practice helps us put things in the right order by teaching us how to *be* before we *do*. When we are coming from that grounded, peaceful place within, we can better take care of what needs to be done. This is what I mean by living from the inside out; we have to live (or be) inwardly and go (or do) outwardly. This is a lifelong practice: *being and then doing*.

From meditation to reflection, The Practice guides us through our day, allowing us the space to truly be ourselves and to live life with purpose and meaning. A beautiful saying goes, "We're not going to pass in this life until we have done what we have come here to do." Thinking about this brings tears to my eyes: *Have I done what I came here to do?*

What is my purpose? is a question most people ask at some point in their lives. I believe that when we go within and take the time to be and listen to our inner voice, our life will beautifully unfold before our eyes, revealing to each of us what it is we have come here to accomplish. For me, I believe that I have come here to know, at a profoundly deep level, that we are all incredible human beings, we are all connected at a deep level of consciousness, and we are all one. I have come here to realize this Truth within myself and to be an instrument of peace and love. I believe that each of us has the capacity to know what our purpose is and to perform it in a meaningful way.

During my life's path, I have experienced many types of people. I love exploring and being open and receptive to all of what life has to offer. Earlier in my life, a tarot card reader once told me, "You already are the person you want so desperately to be. You just don't believe it." Deep down, I knew she was correct. Today I do believe I am who I have always wanted to be: a happy, loving person. Yes, I was once an insecure, unhappy girl, but the woman I am today promises you that when you walk the path for yourself, you will see the love and beauty of life all around you, and that is where you will find your belief in your magnificence.

Toward the end of his life, the literary giant George Bernard Shaw was asked what person in history he would most like to have been. His response was the George Bernard Shaw he might have been. When we go within and discover who we are, we realize this Truth: we are *magnificent* human beings who are capable of doing magnificent things, and we are meant to do magnificent things with our lives. Let us never forget that! Gabrielle Bernstein spoke these words on a retreat my daughter and I attended in 2013, and they evoked in me a resounding *yes*: "Step into the person you are here to be." When we step into who we are here to be by bringing our mind, body, and heart into alignment, we live the life of purpose, love, and confidence that we are here to live.

When my good friend James Finley, a former monk and author, gave a lecture at Florida Atlantic University's Peaceful Mind Peaceful Life Program in January 2010, he said, "As human beings, we are not only meant to survive but *we are meant to thrive.*" What a beautiful way to share this message!

Having a spiritual practice can help us thrive by staying connected to the deep source within that continues to provide us with inspiration for living a mindful, peaceful life. I always like to say, "Don't take life so seriously, but be serious about what you want your life to be." If a peaceful, loving, fulfilling, and purposeful life is what you desire, be serious in your commitment to yourself to follow a spiritual path. No matter what age you are in life, said George Eliot, "It's never too late to be what you might have been."

I would like to conclude this book where I started: with Abraham Lincoln. In 2011, my beautiful friend Doris Kearns Goodwin, a Pulitzer Prize–winning American biographer, historian, and political commentator, spoke at our Festival of the Arts in Boca Raton, Florida. I was captivated by her talk about Lincoln and her book *Team of Rivals: The Political Genius of Abraham Lincoln*. Her ease of relating the stories of "these characters," as she referred to them, and her humor in speaking about Lincoln was incredible. I really felt as if she had lived with them.

Doris concluded her talk by saying Lincoln wanted to live a life worthy of being written about. This touched my heart deeply. I asked myself, *Have I lived a life worthy of being written about?* Not that we need or want to live our lives so that they can be written about, but ask yourself this question as you lie down to sleep tonight: *Am I living the authentic, heartfelt, happy life I wish to live?* This *is* your birthright as a human being, so go within and then go out and live your magnificent life!

APPENDIX A

Sample Sacred Mantras

Aramaic	
Maranatha	Translation: Lord of the heart
Buddhism	
Om Mani Padme Hum *(Aum Mah-nee Pahd-may Hum)*	Translation: Behold! The jewel in the lotus within!
Christianity	
My God and My All	Source: Prayer words of Saint Francis of Assisi
Kyrie Eléison	Translation: Lord have mercy
Jesus	Son of God
Hail Mary/Ave Maria	From the Rosary
O Maria Madre Mia	Translation: Oh Mary My Mother; Source: Prayer words of Pope John Paul II

Lord Jesus Christ, Son of God, Have Mercy on Me	Prayer name: The Jesus Prayer
Be Still and Know That I Am God	From the Bible
Hinduism	
Rama *(Rah-mah)*	Translation: Blissful, pleasing; Source: Mantra of Mahatma Gandhi
Hare Rama Hare Krishna	Translation: O Lord take away all my sorrows, pain, and shortcomings; give me bliss and joy
Om Namah Shivaya *(Aum Num-ha Shi-why)*	Translation: I bow to Shiva—the name of your true identity; self
Om Shanti *(Aum Shan-tee)*	Translation: Lasting peace
So Hum	Translation: I am that Self within
Om Prema	Translation: A call for universal love
Om Sri Ram, Jai Ram, Jai Jai Ram *(Aum Shree Ram, Jay Ram, Jay Jay Ram)*	Translation: May the Lord as light and virtue that dwells in my heart be victorious over all; Source: Mantra of Swami Ramdas
Islam	
Allah	Translation: God
Allahu Akhbar *(Ah-lah-oo Ah-bahr)*	Translation: God is greatest
Bismallah Ir-rahman Ir-rahim *(Beese-mah-lah Ir-rah-mun Ir-rah-heem)*	Translation: In the name of Allah, the Most Beneficent and the Most Merciful

Judaism	
Barukh Hashem *(Bah-rookh ha shem)*	Translation: Blessed is the name
Ribono Shel Olam *(Ree-boh-no Shel O-lahm)*	Translation: Lord of the universe
Shalom	Translation: Lasting peace
Elohim *(e'-lohim)*	Translation: Hebrew name for God
Sheheena	Translation: Feminine aspect of God
Native American Tradition	
Wakan Tanka	Translation: Great Spirit

APPENDIX B

RECOMMENDED
INSPIRATIONAL READING

I have personally read each of the books listed here. My life has been greatly enriched and nourished by these inspiring teachers. My beautiful wish for you is that your hearts will be moved and that you will be inspired to "take the journey" with all who have shared their stories with us.

Ageless Body Timeless Mind by Deepak Chopra

After the Ecstasy, the Laundry: How the Heart Grows Wise on the Spiritual Path by Jack Kornfield

The Alchemist by Paulo Coelho

The Art of Happiness, 10th Anniversary Edition, by His Holiness the Dalai Lama and Howard C. Cutler, M.D.

Autobiography of a Yogi by Paramahansa Yogananda

Cave in the Snow: Tenzin Palmo's Quest for Enlightenment by
Vicki Mackenzie

The Cloud of Unknowing by William Johnston

Concerning the Inner Life by Evelyn Underhill

The Confessions: Saint Augustine by Maria Boulding

The Contemplative Heart by James Finley

Dark Night of the Soul by St. John of the Cross

Empowering Your Soul Through Meditation by Rajinder Singh

The Essential Rumi by Jalal al-Din Rumi

The Four Agreements: A Practical Guide to Personal Freedom
by Don Miguel Ruiz

Francis of Assisi: A Revolutionary Life by Adrian House

The Game of Life and How to Play It by Florence Scovel Shinn

The Gift of Change by Marianne Williamson

God's Fool: The Life and Times of Francis of Assisi by Julien
Green

The Gospel of Sri Ramakrishna by Swami Nikhilananda

Heal Your Body by Louise Hay

*Holy Mother: Being the Wife of Sri Ramakrishna and Helpmate
in His Mission* by Swami Nikhilananda

How to Know God: The Yoga Aphorisms of Patanjali by Swami
Prabhavananda and Christopher Isherwood

Peace Pilgrim: Her Life and Work in Her Own Words/Peace Pilgrim, compiled by Friends of Peace Pilgrim

The Perennial Philosophy: An Interpretation of the Great Mystics, East and West by Aldous Huxley

The Power of Now by Eckhart Tolle

The Practice of the Presence of God by Brother Lawrence

Practicing the Power of Now by Eckhart Tolle

The Prophet by Kahlil Gibran

Ramakrishna and His Disciples by Christopher Isherwood

Reflections on a Mountain Lake: Teachings on Practical Buddhism by Ani Tenzin Palmo

Religions of Man by Huston Smith

A Right to Be Merry by Mother Mary Francis

The Road Less Traveled by M. Scott Peck

Saint Teresa of Avila by Marcelle Auclair

Search Inside Yourself: The Unexpected Path to Achieving Success, Happiness (and World Peace) by Chade-Meng Tan

Seeds of Contemplation by Thomas Merton

The Shadow Effect: Illuminating the Hidden Power of Your True Self by Deepak Chopra, Marianne Williamson, and Debbie Ford

Six Lighted Windows: Memories of Swamis in the West by Swami Yogeshananda

Spirit Junkie by Gabrielle Bernstein

Spontaneous Happiness by Andrew Weil, M.D.

Stillness Speaks by Eckhart Tolle

Tao Te Ching by Lao Tzu

Team of Rivals: The Political Genius of Abraham Lincoln by Doris Kearns Goodwin

They Lived with God: Life Stories of Some Devotees of Sri Ramakrishna by Swami Chetanananda

The Voice of Knowledge: A Practical Guide to Inner Peace by Don Miguel Ruiz

The Way of a Pilgrim by R. M. French

Way of the Peaceful Warrior by Dan Millman

When Things Fall Apart by Pema Chödrön

The Wisdom of Forgiveness by the Dalai Lama and Victor Chan

The Yoga Sutras of Patanjali by Sri Swami Satchidananda

You Are Here: Discovering the Magic of the Present Moment by Thich Nhat Hanh

———

The following are representative works from the great religions that I have found inspirational:

The Bhagavad Gita	The Koran (Qur'an)
The Bible	The Torah
The Dhammapada	The Upanishads

ACKNOWLEDGMENTS

Writing this book was a labor of love. I have been giving workshops and lectures on the topic of peaceful living for over a decade. When my friends and family said, "Barb, you should write a book," I thought, *Sure, why not!* Little did I realize the commitment and time a project like this would take and the true necessity of patience and love from everyone around me. I offer my heartfelt gratitude to everyone who supported me, loved me, and held me during this beautiful process.

Michelle Maros, the day you were born you taught me patience and the very meaning of selfless service. As the Peaceful Mind Peaceful Life creative director, and primary contributing writer for the blogs, you are truly stepping into the magnificent person you came here to be. I am so proud to be your mom. You are beautiful and loving, and you are my greatest blessing. I love you, precious daughter.

For Dick Schmidt, my loving husband, friend, and "the person I would most want to be in a foxhole with"! My love and gratitude are yours for helping me to grow into a person who loves herself and her life. You have supported me in a way that touches my heart so deeply, and I look forward to sharing that porch swing with you. I love you, sweetie.

To Jetsunma Tenzin Palmo, James Finley, Gabrielle Bernstein, Doris Kearns Goodwin, Dan Baker, Coach Howard Schnellenberger, and Noemi Marin; you are my friends, my teachers, and a source of true inspiration. I give you my heart full of thanks and a big hug for so beautifully and lovingly endorsing this book and my work. Together, we share love, peace, and light with the world. I love you.

To my other teachers who have profoundly touched my life and my work, a thank you hardly seems enough: His Holiness the Dalai Lama, Thich Nhat Hanh, Deepak Chopra, Caroline Myss, Pema Chödrön, and Marianne Williamson; you have taught me how to go within to deeply connect with my Beloved. To all the great saints, masters, and mystics from many of the world's traditions and religions; your teachings have changed, enriched, and nourished my life.

I send into the Universe a thank you to my mom and dad, Rosemary and Chuck Andres, and my husband's parents,

Dorothy and Chuck Schmidt. Mom and Dad, thank you for giving me life; if it were not for you, I would not be here fulfilling my deep desire to bring peace and love to the world. I love you. To Dorothy and Chuck, you raised a brilliant, loving son and because of your generosity of heart, through your Schmidt Family Foundation, as a Trustee, I have learned deeply the responsibility, love, and joy of giving to others in a really big way. Thank you for this teaching and for your son.

My love and heartfelt thanks to my grandfather, Harry Andres, for all of the summers in the garage, in the garden, and walking to mass; you gave me attention, love, and value as a child. You may well be my greatest teacher!

For David Schmidt and Chris Stafford, you have given me your love, advice, and sweet friendship. I am forever grateful for having you in my life. Thank you for being a sounding board for many of the ideas presented in this book and in my work. Love to you always.

To my beautiful sister, Carolyn Hallanger. Even though I am the oldest, you have always looked over me and supported me the way a "big sister" would. But you are more than a sister; you are my forever friend. When we were growing up and I needed a friend, you were always there for me just as you are today. I love you.

To my brothers, Chuck, Tom, and Ed Andres. I am proud of you and of the lives you are leading! My beautiful sisters-in-law, my amazing nieces and nephews, and the three of you have given me tremendous support in launching Peaceful Mind Peaceful Life into the world through social media. Although we don't see each other often, you are part of my heart; this gives me great comfort and joy. I love you.

A big thank you from my heart to Gloria Pierson. I appreciate you, Gloria, for "always having my back," for your steadfast loyalty, and for your strong personal practice and convictions in helping to bring the work of Peaceful Mind Peaceful Life to this great place.

Much love and thanks to my "spiritual family and meditation friends." Almost every Tuesday night for the past fifteen years, we have been inspired by one another and meditated together with the intention of bringing love and peace to our lives and the world. I love you all!

My deep heartfelt thanks and my love are hardly enough for you, Adriana Faraldo. Your friendship, love, and our beautiful times together are forever part of my being.

Carmen Knight, your expertise in laying the groundwork for Peaceful Mind Peaceful Life as a "brand" and movement in the world was remarkable; my love and thanks go out to you, my friend.

To Maria Levix, Judy Loglisci, and Olimpia Perez; my love and thanks are yours for always being there for me, unconditionally, with a smile and a loving heart and hand.

Thank you, Carolyn Cunningham, for introducing me to yoga. This practice has been a pure blessing in my life, as have you.

Big thanks to Lesley Marlo, David Schmidt, and Becky Remmel. The three of you were there in the beginning, patient and steadfast, as we launched Peaceful Mind Peaceful Life to the world.

To Catherine Schmidt; you are strong, supportive, loving, and protective of me. Thank you, and my love to you always, my friend.

To Laurie Carney of the Dorothy F. Schmidt College of Arts and Letters at Florida Atlantic University and Noemi Marin of the Peace Studies Program; my thanks and love for always being my "cheerleaders" and friends. Thank you, Polly Burks, Nicole Jacobsen, Gail Vorsas, and Audra Vaz. You all have given me so much attention and help as we presented my workshops to the community over the past ten years.

Thank you, Dawn Stevenson Arnold, my beautiful "roomie" and friend, my lasting love to you.

To Carol Killman Rosenberg; when I asked my publisher to recommend writers and editors for this project, I could not have imagined my great fortune in finding you. From the moment we spoke, we connected. I shared with you my deepest stories and you helped guide me in the development of content, writing, editing, and flow. Our back-and-forth process expertly shaped the manuscript into the book it is today. More than all of this (and it's a whole lot!), you are my friend. You are smart, patient, and gentle, and I thank you from the bottom of my heart for this beautiful finished product. Much love.

For Gary Rosenberg, thank you for your incredibly beautiful and speedy layout of flyers, ads, and most importantly The Practice workbooks. They are gorgeous and practical and have supported my workshops and retreats in such a deep, meaningful way.

Thank you, Robin Gilbertson, for your many illustrations of our Peaceful Mind Peaceful Life dandelion logo; your patience was perfect. And to Jessica Chin Fong, thank you for putting the final touches on our incredibly beautiful logo and for designing the powerful illustration of the mind in this book, which I use for almost every talk I give.

My love and thanks to Terra Spero Malone and RealTime Marketing Group. You have taken Peaceful Mind Peaceful Life to the social-media masses in a way that is unbelievable! Our growth means more people are inspired to be peaceful and loving, so in this way, we are changing the world one person at a time—my deepest desire! Your love, dedication, and the creative work by your team, Chris Cuccia and Irin Akter, have sparked confidence in everyone, and we are having great fun!

I wish to thank the staff at HCI Books for their support, expertise, and kindness. To Peter Vegso, my publisher; thank you for providing me with the wonderful opportunity to get my book out into the world where it can reach a wider audience of readers and seekers. To my editor at HCI Books, Christine Belleris; I appreciate your taking an interest in this project and shepherding it with such a loving hand through the publishing process. To designer Larissa Henoch; thank you for your patience, laughter, and thoughtfulness, and for giving me the space to be creative and "play" with you in the creation of the book cover. To PR director, Kim Weiss; thank you for masterfully heading up the promotional efforts for this book. And to all the behind-the-scenes staff who have played an integral role in the publication of this book, I thank you all from deep within my heart.

Many thanks to Jenna Guarneri and the entire PR team at Sarah Hall PR for believing in this book and in me and for brilliantly sharing my message of love and peace with the world. It was awesome to guide you in a meditation after our very first meeting. You are all so very special.

So much love and thanks to my Boca Raton Community Friends. You are my family, my "A" Team, and I love you all. Big thanks to every person who has attended my workshops, lectures, and retreats. Your support and love for my work and for me all these years means more to me that I can express on this page.

ABOUT THE AUTHOR

Barb Schmidt is a businesswoman, philanthropist, and spiritual coach with over thirty years devoted to spiritual development and research. She has studied with Thich Nhat Hanh, Deepak Chopra, Scott Peck, and Marianne Williamson, among many other notable teachers. As founder of Spirit of Giving Network and cofounder and past president of Ronald McDonald Children's Charities of South Florida, Barb raised millions of dollars for children and families in need.

In 2001, Barb partnered with Florida Atlantic University's Peace Studies Program to promote dialogue in the greater community on the topic of peace. Additionally, she taught a class on meditation and spiritual practices as part of the lifelong learning program at Nova University for five years. For the past ten years, she has been offering quarterly workshops and weekly classes on spiritual practices and has facilitated lectures by many notable speakers, including the Dalai Lama, Dr. Jane Goodall, Caroline Myss, James Finley, Ph.D., Dr. Mona Lisa Schultz, Dan Millman, and Gabrielle Bernstein. A sought-after speaker herself, Barb regularly lectures at schools and organizations to spread her message of living a meaningful, happy life.

In 2011, Barb founded Peaceful Mind Peaceful Life through which she teaches The Practice—a three-part guide to practical spirituality in today's modern world. A well-respected nonprofit, Peaceful Mind Peaceful Life has quickly expanded to include an online community via Facebook and through the daily blog at *www.peacefulmindpeacefullife.com*.

Barb lives in Boca Raton, Florida, with her husband, Dick, and is the mother of Michelle and David. For more information, visit *www.barbschmidt.com*.

ABOUT
PEACEFUL MIND
PEACEFUL LIFE

SHARING A VISION OF CHANGING THE WORLD THROUGH INNER PEACE

Peaceful Mind Peaceful Life is a non-profit organization, resource, and community helping people incorporate into their lives spiritual tools that promote a peaceful mind and a happy, loving, and peaceful life. Founded in 2011 by philanthropist and lifelong seeker, Barb Schmidt, Peaceful Mind Peaceful Life serves as an ongoing support system, teacher, advisor, and friend to guide you along the path of living from within.

Through spiritual disciplines like The Practice and a wealth of spiritual wisdom from other revered teachers, the Peaceful Mind Peaceful Life community and friends are invited to learn more about time-tested methods of self-empowerment, stress management, inner peace, and selfless service.

Join the movement of bringing peace and love to our households, schools, communities, and world by learning how you can become a Peacemaker "from the inside out." Visit *www.peacefulmindpeacefullife.org.* Enjoy the blog at *peacefulmindpeacefullife.org/blog*, follow the organization on Twitter at *twitter.com/wakeupandstop*, and "like" the Peaceful Mind Peaceful Life Facebook page.

THE MEANING
BEHIND THE
DANDELION

*"The real voyage of discovery
consists not in seeking new lands
but seeing with new eyes."*

—Marcel Proust

I'd like to leave you with a brief explanation of the dandelion associated with Peaceful Mind Peaceful Life. Being familiar with the significance of this simple flower will help you to better appreciate the mission of this wonderful organization.

♦ ♦ ♦

As a child, I loved the dandelions growing on our lawn. And like most children, I enjoyed blowing the seeds into the wind and seeing them take flight to land somewhere far, far away. When it was my turn to mow the grass, my dad would say, "Mow those dandelions, too. They're just weeds," but I really didn't want to mow them down. I just thought they were so pretty, especially the seed part. I still do. And I love that the dandelion is the Peaceful Mind Peaceful Life logo.

When we were looking for a logo to represent the spiritual life, we considered several options—and although there were many good ideas, none quite fit the bill. The search continued for several months until we arrived at the dandelion as a serious consideration. Could it be that something so ordinary and abundant could be what we were seeking?

It turns out that it was exactly what we were seeking: A spiritual life is often found in the ordinary. We search for it all over the place, but it has always been right there in front of us, and there is an abundant supply. We have a tendency to overlook the common. What could better symbolize this than the dandelion? It is so simple, and it is everywhere! When we dug deeper into the qualities of the dandelion, we discovered that although it seems ordinary, the dandelion has so many wonderful properties:

- ⤱ A dandelion can grow in just about any place. It can survive even in the roughest environments.
- ⤱ The dandelion has a deep root system that gives it the strength to withstand just about anything.
- ⤱ The dandelion is filled with health-promoting nutrients. Yes, you can eat them.
- ⤱ Dandelions have medicinal properties and can be used by holistic doctors to treat many ailments.
- ⤱ The dandelion's transformation from flower to seed is a promise that it will continue to live on.
- ⤱ Dandelion seeds spread far and wide—you never know where they will take root.

These qualities of the dandelion can easily be applied to the spiritual life. The spiritual life is our ordinary, daily life. It is right there in front of us all the time. It gives us strength to withstand just about anything—even unfriendly environments; it nourishes our being and heals us when necessary; it shows us that transformation is beneficial and that we never know where our seeds—our spiritual legacy—will take root.

My friend Cathy wrote to us recently to say, "The dandelion is almost like a secret password for those who have attended your workshops. Its simplicity and understatedness speak volumes about those who choose to make time for peace in their minds, hearts, and lives."

In this way, the dandelion can be the password you use to unlock the door within that has been waiting patiently for you to open it.

INDEX